Game Development with Python: Learn by Creating Your First 2D Game

A Step-by-Step Guide to Building Games with Python

BOOZMAN RICHARD

BOOKER BLUNT

Table of Content

TABLE OF CONTENTS

INTRODUCTION

The Game development landscape has evolved dramatically over the past decade, with python frameworks playing a pivotal role in shaping how developers build interactive, dynamic, and scalable applications. In this rapidly changing ecosystem, staying up to date with the latest frameworks and technologies is crucial to building high-performance web applications that meet user expectations for speed, reliability, and seamless experiences across devices.

This book, *Mastering JavaScript Frameworks: From React to Angular*, is designed to be your comprehensive guide to mastering the most popular JavaScript frameworks used in modern web development. Whether you are just starting your journey into web development or you're a seasoned developer looking to deepen your knowledge, this book covers everything you need to know about **React**, **Angular**, and **Vue.js**. Each chapter is crafted to provide you with a clear understanding of the core concepts, best practices, and real-world examples, helping you build scalable, maintainable, and performant applications.

Why This Book Is Essential

The demand for rich, interactive web applications has never been higher. With the rise of Single Page Applications (SPAs), Progressive Web Apps (PWAs), and mobile-first design, developers must not only understand the principles of front-end development but also leverage modern JavaScript frameworks to enhance the user experience and meet the growing demands of today's digital world.

In this book, you will:

- Gain a deep understanding of **React**, **Angular**, and **Vue.js**, each of which has its unique strengths and weaknesses.
- Learn how to implement best practices for building fast, efficient, and secure web applications.
- Dive into advanced topics such as **state management**, **routing**, **service workers**, and **performance optimization**.
- Explore real-world examples of building web apps from scratch, including integrating APIs, securing user data, and optimizing performance.

- Get hands-on experience with building **Progressive Web Apps (PWAs), Single Page Applications (SPAs)**, and mobile-first web solutions.

Whether you're looking to improve your skills in building scalable front-end applications or need to stay updated with the latest trends and technologies in web development, this book will serve as your essential companion.

What You Will Learn

In the first part of the book, we'll explore the foundational concepts of JavaScript frameworks. You'll get acquainted with the core principles behind **React**, **Angular**, and **Vue.js**, including their strengths, weaknesses, and appropriate use cases. We'll dive into the fundamentals of each framework, helping you choose the right tool for your next project.

Next, we will cover how to build real-world applications with these frameworks. You'll learn how to develop powerful web apps by creating dynamic user interfaces, managing state effectively, and implementing modern features like **routing**, **authentication**, and **data binding**. You'll also get hands-on experience building **single-page**

applications (SPAs) and integrating APIs to enhance the functionality of your app.

As we move deeper into advanced topics, the book will guide you through **state management** using libraries like **Redux** for React, **NgRx** for Angular, and **Vuex** for Vue.js. We'll also focus on performance optimization techniques such as **code splitting, lazy loading, caching**, and **progressive web apps (PWAs)** to ensure that your web apps perform at their best across all devices and network conditions.

Security is also a major concern when developing web applications. In this book, we'll explore how to protect your app from common vulnerabilities like **Cross-Site Scripting (XSS), Cross-Site Request Forgery (CSRF)**, and **SQL Injection**. You'll learn how to implement secure authentication systems using **JWT** (JSON Web Tokens) and other modern techniques to safeguard your app's data and user privacy.

The final section of the book covers best practices and strategies for maintaining and evolving your web apps. We'll focus on **test-driven development (TDD), unit testing**, and **end-to-end testing** with tools like **Jest, Karma,** and **Protractor**. We'll also discuss how to stay up to date with the latest trends and frameworks in the JavaScript ecosystem, ensuring your skills remain relevant in the ever-changing world of web development.

Who This Book Is For

This book is intended for developers of all experience levels who want to master modern JavaScript frameworks. Whether you are:

- A **beginner** looking to get started with React, Angular, or Vue.js, and want to learn the fundamentals of web development with modern frameworks.
- An **intermediate developer** who wants to deepen your understanding of state management, routing, testing, and performance optimization.
- An **experienced developer** seeking to stay updated on the latest tools, best practices, and trends in JavaScript frameworks, and how to build scalable, secure, and high-performance web applications.

Why React, Angular, and Vue.js?

The three frameworks covered in this book—**React, Angular**, and **Vue.js**—are the most widely used and popular choices for building web applications today. Each framework has unique features, and understanding their strengths and use cases will help you choose the right one for your project.

- **React**: Known for its simplicity and flexibility, React is a **JavaScript library** for building user interfaces. Its component-based architecture and virtual DOM make it highly efficient for rendering dynamic UIs, and it is widely adopted for creating modern, fast web applications.

- **Angular**: Angular is a **full-fledged framework** that provides everything you need for building large-scale web applications. With built-in tools like **dependency injection**, **routing**, and **forms management**, Angular is perfect for building complex, enterprise-level apps.

- **Vue.js**: Vue is a **progressive framework** that is both easy to learn and flexible enough to scale for large applications. It combines the best features of both React and Angular, offering an approachable

11

learning curve with powerful tools for building dynamic, modern web apps.

By the end of this book, you'll have a solid understanding of these frameworks and the ability to build robust, production-ready web apps with them.

Conclusion

The world of JavaScript frameworks is constantly evolving, and staying up-to-date with the latest tools and techniques is essential for becoming a proficient game developer. *With python s: From React to Angular* offers a detailed, hands-on guide to building modern web applications that are fast, scalable, and secure. By mastering these frameworks, you'll be equipped to tackle any web development challenge and stay at the forefront of the ever-changing landscape of web technologies.

Whether you're building a personal project or working on an enterprise-level application, the skills and knowledge you gain from this book will serve as a solid foundation for your future web development career. Let's dive in and explore the power of **React**, **Angular**, and **Vue.js**, and start building modern web apps that users love!

CHAPTER 1

INTRODUCTION TO GAME DEVELOPMENT WITH PYTHON

Overview of Game Development Basics

Game development involves creating software that allows users to interact with virtual environments. At its core, game development is about building systems that manage user input, display graphics, and produce an interactive experience. A successful game requires not only coding skills but also a solid understanding of game mechanics, design principles, and how to keep players engaged.

While the technical aspects, such as the programming languages and frameworks, are critical, the game development process also involves creativity in designing characters, levels, and challenges that make the game fun. For this reason, game development is often a blend of art and science.

Introduction to Python as a Game Development Language

Python has gained popularity as a game development language due to its simplicity and ease of use. While many professional games are built with languages like C++ or C#, Python is

13

particularly suited for smaller projects, prototyping, and learning how to make games. It's versatile, well-documented, and has a wide range of libraries that help speed up the development process.

In this book, we will use Python to create a 2D game. Python's straightforward syntax makes it an ideal choice for beginners who are just stepping into the world of game development. You won't need to worry about complex memory management or low-level code—Python allows you to focus more on the fun part of game creation.

Installing Python and the Necessary Libraries (Pygame)

Before you start building games, you need to install Python and some essential libraries. Python can be downloaded from its official website (https://www.python.org). Once installed, you can use the terminal or command prompt to verify the installation by typing:

```bash

python --version
```

This should return the version of Python that you installed. The next step is to install Pygame, a popular library for creating 2D games with Python. Pygame simplifies game development by handling common tasks such as displaying graphics, managing sounds, and handling input devices.

To install Pygame, open your terminal or command prompt and run:

```bash

pip install pygame
```

Once Pygame is installed, you can start creating your first game!

Understanding the Game Development Workflow

The game development process can be broken down into several key stages. Here's an overview of the typical workflow:

1. **Concept and Design**: In this initial phase, you brainstorm the idea for your game. What type of game do you want to create? Is it a platformer, puzzle, or adventure game? You'll also sketch out the story, characters, and mechanics that define the game experience.

2. **Prototyping**: Once you have a design in mind, it's time to build a simple version of the game. This prototype allows you to test core mechanics (such as movement or collision detection) and see if your ideas work in practice. It's common to iterate on this prototype several times before moving to more complex features.

3. **Development**: This is where the bulk of the coding happens. You'll implement features such as game mechanics, artificial intelligence, and level design. Development often involves a lot of testing and debugging.

4. **Polishing**: After the game's core mechanics are working, it's time to refine the game. This includes adding better graphics, sound effects, animations, and improving user interface (UI) elements.

5. **Testing and Feedback**: At this stage, you playtest the game to find bugs and improve gameplay. Feedback from others is essential to fine-tuning the user experience.

6. **Release**: Once the game is polished, tested, and ready, it can be released to the public. Whether through an online platform or a downloadable file, you'll share your game with others to enjoy.

The Importance of Game Loops, Frames, and Event Handling

To understand how games work at a basic level, you need to be familiar with key concepts like game loops, frames, and event handling.

- **Game Loop**: The game loop is the backbone of every game. It runs continuously and handles all the tasks needed to keep the game running. The game loop involves three main steps:

16

1. **Handle events**: The game listens for input, such as mouse clicks or keyboard presses.
2. **Update the game state**: The game logic, such as character movement, collision detection, or physics, is processed.
3. **Render the game**: The graphics are drawn to the screen, and the game state is displayed.

Each iteration of the game loop is called a frame, and the smoother and faster the frames are rendered, the more fluid the game feels.

- **Frames**: Frames represent the individual pictures that are displayed on the screen as part of the game's animation. A typical game runs at around 30-60 frames per second (FPS), depending on how smooth and responsive you want the gameplay to feel. The higher the FPS, the smoother the game's movement and animations.
- **Event Handling**: Game events are the interactions between the user and the game. Examples include pressing a key to move a character or clicking the mouse to fire a weapon. Event handling ensures that the game responds appropriately to user actions.

In this chapter, you will gain an understanding of these fundamental concepts. We will build on these concepts throughout the book as we dive deeper into creating your first 2D game with Python.

By the end of this chapter, you'll have a basic understanding of how game loops work, how to install Python and Pygame, and how to begin your journey into the exciting world of game development!

CHAPTER 2

SETTING UP YOUR DEVELOPMENT ENVIRONMENT

In this chapter, we'll guide you through the steps required to set up your development environment for Python game development. This involves installing Python, Pygame, and necessary dependencies, setting up a code editor, and writing your first Python script to test the environment.

Step-by-Step Guide to Installing Pygame and Other Dependencies

Before you can start writing your first game, you need to ensure that your development environment is set up properly. Here's how to get everything ready:

1. **Install Python**

   Python is the core programming language for our game development project. If you haven't installed Python yet, follow these steps:

o Go to the official Python website and download the latest version for your operating system (Windows, macOS, or Linux).

o Follow the installation instructions, making sure to check the option that says **"Add Python to PATH"** during installation. This ensures you can run Python from any terminal window.

After installing, you can verify Python is installed by opening your terminal or command prompt and typing:

```
bash
```

```
python --version
```

This will display the Python version installed on your machine.

2. **Install Pygame**

Pygame is a library that simplifies game development with Python. It helps you handle images, sounds, events, and other aspects of game development.

To install Pygame, open your terminal or command prompt and enter the following command:

```
bash
```

```
pip install pygame
```

The `pip` command is Python's package installer, and this will download and install the Pygame library on your system. To ensure Pygame was installed successfully, you can run:

```
bash
```

```
python -m pygame.examples.aliens
```

If the installation was successful, a small game demo will run.

3. **Other Dependencies**

In most games, you might need additional dependencies such as image libraries or audio tools. However, Pygame is often sufficient for building simple 2D games. If you plan on adding extra features (like 3D rendering, physics simulations, etc.), you may need to install additional libraries later on.

Setting Up a Code Editor

To write Python code, you'll need a code editor or an integrated development environment (IDE). Two popular choices for Python development are **Visual Studio Code** (VSCode) and **PyCharm**. Here's how to set them up:

1. **Visual Studio Code (VSCode)**

   VSCode is a lightweight, free, and highly customizable code editor that works well for Python development.

   - **Download and Install VSCode**: Visit the official website and download the appropriate version for your operating system.
   - **Install Python Extension**: After installing VSCode, open it, and go to the Extensions tab (on the left sidebar). Search for the "Python" extension by Microsoft and click Install. This extension adds Python-specific features like syntax highlighting, debugging support, and auto-completion.
   - **Configure VSCode**: Open a folder where you plan to save your projects, and start a new Python file. You'll now be ready to write Python code and run it directly within VSCode.

2. **PyCharm**

   PyCharm is another great option for Python development, and it provides many advanced features like a built-in debugger, database tools, and testing support. There are two versions: the free **Community Edition** and the paid **Professional Edition**.

- o **Download and Install PyCharm**: Visit the official website and download the appropriate version for your operating system.
- o **Set Up Python Interpreter**: When you first launch PyCharm, it will ask you to configure the Python interpreter. Make sure to choose the Python version you installed earlier.
- o **Start Coding**: Once PyCharm is set up, you can start creating new Python files, write your code, and run it directly from the editor.

Both VSCode and PyCharm are excellent choices, but if you're new to coding, VSCode is an excellent lightweight option to start with. If you plan to work on larger projects or need advanced features, PyCharm could be a better choice.

Exploring the Pygame Library and Its Key Modules

Now that your environment is set up, let's dive into **Pygame**. The Pygame library is split into different modules, each serving a specific purpose for game development. Here are the most important ones you'll be working with:

1. **pygame.display**: Manages the game window and the graphical output. You use this module to create a window for your game, set its title, and control its dimensions.

2. **pygame.image**: Used to load, display, and manipulate images (such as sprites and backgrounds). This is one of the most commonly used modules in game development.

3. **pygame.mixer**: Handles sound effects and background music. It allows you to load and play audio files (like `.mp3`, `.wav`, etc.).

4. **pygame.event**: This module is used to handle events, such as keyboard presses, mouse clicks, and window resizing. It's central to managing interactions between the player and the game.

5. **pygame.sprite**: Manages sprites, which are the visual elements of your game. It allows you to create and manage multiple sprites efficiently.

6. **pygame.time**: Helps you control time-related tasks, such as frame rate and the game clock. It's essential for ensuring smooth animations and gameplay.

7. **pygame.rect**: Defines rectangular areas for handling positioning and collision detection of game objects.

Writing Your First Python Script to Test the Environment

Now that you've installed Python, Pygame, and set up your editor, it's time to write a basic Python script to test everything.

Here's a simple script that creates a game window and fills it with a color:

```python
python

import pygame
import sys

# Initialize Pygame
pygame.init()

# Set up the game window
screen = pygame.display.set_mode((800, 600))   #
width=800px, height=600px
pygame.display.set_caption("My First Game")

# Define the game colors
WHITE = (255, 255, 255)
BLUE = (0, 0, 255)

# Main game loop
while True:
    # Handle events
    for event in pygame.event.get():
        if event.type == pygame.QUIT:
            pygame.quit()
            sys.exit()

    # Fill the screen with a color
```

```
screen.fill(WHITE)

# Draw a blue rectangle
pygame.draw.rect(screen, BLUE, (350, 250,
100, 100))  # (x, y, width, height)

# Update the screen
pygame.display.update()
```

This script does the following:

- Initializes Pygame and sets up an 800x600 window.
- Sets the window's title to "My First Game."
- Enters a game loop where it listens for the quit event (when you close the window).
- Fills the window with a white color and draws a blue rectangle in the center.
- Updates the window to show the changes.

To run this, save the script as `first_game.py` and execute it from your terminal or command prompt:

```bash
```

```
python first_game.py
```

If everything is set up correctly, a window should appear with a white background and a blue rectangle in the middle.

Conclusion

In this chapter, you learned how to set up your development environment, install Python and Pygame, and create your first Python script to test the setup. By the end of this chapter, you should have a solid foundation for starting your journey into game development with Python. In the next chapters, we'll build on this setup, diving deeper into creating actual game mechanics and enhancing your skills further.

CHAPTER 3

INTRODUCTION TO PYGAME: THE BASICS

In this chapter, we'll introduce **Pygame**, a powerful library for building games with Python. We'll explore its core components, how to set up a game window, and how to work with basic shapes and events like keyboard and mouse inputs. By the end of this chapter, you'll have the foundation to start creating your own 2D games.

What is Pygame and Why It's Great for 2D Game Development

Pygame is a free and open-source set of Python modules that make it easy to develop **2D games** and multimedia applications. It is built on top of **SDL** (Simple DirectMedia Layer), which provides low-level access to audio, keyboard, mouse, and display hardware. Pygame's high-level interface makes it accessible to beginners while still offering enough flexibility for more advanced users.

Why Pygame is Great for 2D Game Development:

28

- **Ease of Use**: Pygame has a simple API that allows you to quickly create games with minimal code.
- **Cross-Platform**: Games built with Pygame can run on Windows, macOS, and Linux, making it an excellent choice for developers who want to reach a wide audience.
- **Great Community and Resources**: There's a vast community of developers, tutorials, and documentation available to help you get started and solve problems.
- **Efficient for 2D Games**: Pygame's focus is on 2D game development, making it perfect for projects that involve simple mechanics, 2D graphics, and animations.

While Pygame isn't typically used for complex 3D games, it's a fantastic choice for beginners looking to learn game development and for developers working on 2D games, prototypes, or educational projects.

Understanding the Core Components: Surfaces, Rectangles, and Images

Pygame is built around several core components that will form the backbone of your game. Understanding these components is essential for creating games efficiently.

1. **Surfaces**:

   A **surface** in Pygame represents an area where graphics

are drawn. It can be thought of as a blank canvas where you can draw shapes, images, and text. The screen itself is also a surface, and you'll use this to render everything you see in the game.

You can create surfaces of any size, and they can be filled with colors, images, or transparency. You'll often use surfaces to represent elements like the player character, obstacles, backgrounds, and projectiles.

Example:

python

```
surface = pygame.Surface((200, 150))   #
Create a surface of 200x150
surface.fill((255, 0, 0))   # Fill the
surface with a red color
```

2. **Rectangles**:

A **rectangle** is an object that defines a position and a size (width and height). Pygame provides a `Rect` class that's used to create rectangular areas. You can use it for various purposes, such as positioning elements on the screen, handling collisions, and setting boundaries for movement.

A `Rect` object is often used with surfaces to determine where to draw something or how to move objects around the screen. You can also use rectangles for collision detection, such as when checking if one object overlaps with another.

Example:

```python
```

```python
player_rect = pygame.Rect(50, 50, 64, 64)
# Position the player at (50, 50), with a
size of 64x64
```

3. **Images**:

Pygame supports image files, such as .jpg, .png, and .bmp, which you can load onto surfaces. Images are typically used for more complex graphics, such as sprites, backgrounds, and other visual elements in the game.

You can load an image using Pygame's pygame.image.load() function, and then render it onto the screen.

Example:

```python
```

```python
image = pygame.image.load('player.png')  #
Load an image of the player character
```

31

```
screen.blit(image,   (player_x,   player_y))
# Draw the image at the player's position
```

Setting Up the Game Window, Display, and Basic Shapes

To start building your game, the first step is to set up a game window where all your gameplay will occur. Pygame provides simple functions for creating a window and displaying graphics.

1. **Setting up the Game Window**: Pygame's `pygame.display.set_mode()` function creates the game window, where all your game graphics will be shown. The size of the window is determined by the argument you pass (in pixels).

   Example:

   ```python
   screen   =   pygame.display.set_mode((800,
   600))  # Creates a window of 800x600 pixels
   pygame.display.set_caption("My       First
   Game")  # Set the window title
   ```

2. **Basic Shapes**: Pygame allows you to draw basic shapes such as rectangles, circles, and lines. These shapes are drawn directly on the screen using the `pygame.draw` module.

32

For example, to draw a simple rectangle or circle on the screen:

- o **Rectangle**:

python

```
pygame.draw.rect(screen,    (255,    0,
0), (50, 50, 200, 150))   # Draw a red
rectangle
```

- o **Circle**:

python

```
pygame.draw.circle(screen,   (0,   255,
0), (400, 300), 50   # Draw a green
circle at (400, 300) with radius 50
```

These basic shapes are helpful for testing and visualizing the layout of your game world, especially as you begin adding more complex elements like characters and objects.

Handling Events: Keyboard, Mouse, and Window Events

One of the fundamental aspects of game development is **event handling**. Events are actions or occurrences that the game listens for and responds to. Pygame provides a simple event loop to handle different types of events, including user inputs from the keyboard and mouse, as well as window events (like closing the window).

1. **Keyboard** **Events**:

   Keyboard events allow players to interact with the game by pressing keys. You can detect key presses, key releases, and the holding of keys using `pygame.event.get()` and checking for specific key events (e.g., `pygame.KEYDOWN`).

Example:

python

```
for event in pygame.event.get():
    if event.type == pygame.QUIT:  # If the
window is closed
        running = False
    elif event.type == pygame.KEYDOWN:
        if event.key == pygame.K_LEFT:  #
Left arrow key pressed
            player_x -= 5 # Move player to
the left
        elif event.key == pygame.K_RIGHT:
# Right arrow key pressed
            player_x += 5 # Move player to
the right
```

34

2. **Mouse** **Events**:

Mouse events allow players to click or move the mouse to interact with the game. Pygame can detect mouse clicks, movements, and even the position of the mouse cursor.

Example:

python

```
for event in pygame.event.get():
    if              event.type              ==
pygame.MOUSEBUTTONDOWN:
        if event.button == 1:  # Left mouse
button
            mouse_x, mouse_y = event.pos  #
Get the mouse position
            print(f"Mouse    clicked    at
{mouse_x}, {mouse_y}")
```

3. **Window** **Events**:

Pygame also handles window events, such as the user closing the game window. The pygame.QUIT event is fired when the user clicks the close button on the window.

Example:

python

```
for event in pygame.event.get():
```

35

```
if event.type == pygame.QUIT:
        pygame.quit()   # Quit the game if
the window is closed
        sys.exit()
```

Conclusion

In this chapter, you've learned the basics of **Pygame** and how it facilitates 2D game development with Python. We covered core components like **surfaces**, **rectangles**, and **images**, which are essential for building your game. You also learned how to set up the **game window**, draw **basic shapes**, and handle user **keyboard**, **mouse**, and **window events**.

By understanding these fundamental components, you're now equipped to start creating your own 2D games. In the next chapters, we'll dive deeper into more advanced game mechanics, such as player movement, collisions, and AI. Keep experimenting with these basics to build a strong foundation as you move forward in your game development journey!

CHAPTER 4

UNDERSTANDING GAME LOOP AND FRAMES

In this chapter, we will dive into one of the most crucial concepts in game development: the **game loop**. The game loop is the heart of any game, constantly running to handle the game's events, update its state, and render new frames on the screen. We'll break down the concept in simple terms, explain how it works, and show you how to implement and optimize it in Python using Pygame.

Explaining the Game Loop in Simple Terms

At its core, the **game loop** is a continuous cycle that keeps the game running. It handles the flow of the game by repeating several key tasks in a specific order:

1. **Event Handling**: The game loop checks if the player has interacted with the game, like pressing a key, moving the mouse, or closing the window. These interactions are captured as events.

2. **Updating the Game State**: Once the game loop has captured all the events, it updates the game's internal

state. For example, it moves the player character, checks for collisions, or updates the score.

3. **Rendering the Scene**: After updating the game state, the loop refreshes the screen, drawing the current state of the game (e.g., the player's position, obstacles, enemies, etc.).

4. **Repetition**: This entire cycle repeats itself many times per second, providing the smooth, interactive experience that players expect in a game.

Think of the game loop as the engine that drives the game, constantly handling input, updating logic, and rendering frames until the player exits the game.

How the Game Loop Manages Events, Updates, and Rendering

In more detail, the game loop consists of three main parts: **event handling**, **game updates**, and **rendering**.

1. **Event   Handling**:
   During the game loop, the game checks for any user inputs (such as key presses, mouse movements, or window actions like closing the game). These are captured as events and are processed in the loop. The game responds to these events by performing corresponding actions, such as moving the player or firing a weapon.

In Pygame, event handling is done using `pygame.event.get()`. The event loop checks all the events that occurred during the current iteration of the game loop and handles them appropriately.

Example:

```python
```

```python
for event in pygame.event.get():
    if event.type == pygame.QUIT:
        running = False
    if event.type == pygame.KEYDOWN:
        if event.key == pygame.K_LEFT:
            player_x -= 5
        elif event.key == pygame.K_RIGHT:
            player_x += 5
```

2. **Game**   **Updates**:

After handling the events, the game updates the state of the game world. This includes updating the position of the player, moving enemies, checking for collisions, and adjusting scores. The game's internal logic (such as physics, artificial intelligence, or level progression) is executed here.

Example:

```python
```

```
player_rect.x += player_speed  # Update the
player's position based on speed
if player_rect.colliderect(enemy_rect):
    player_lives -= 1  # Deduct a life if
the player collides with an enemy
```

3. **Rendering   the   Scene**:
   After updating the game state, the game needs to display the new state to the player. This is done by **rendering** everything on the screen. Pygame uses **surfaces** to draw everything: the background, characters, enemies, and other game elements. After drawing all elements, the screen is updated with `pygame.display.update()` to show the new frame.

   Example:

   python

```
screen.fill((0, 0, 0))  # Fill the screen
with black color
screen.blit(player_image, player_rect)  #
Draw the player image at the updated
position
pygame.display.update()  # Update the
screen to display the new frame
```

Implementing the Game Loop in Python Using Pygame

Now that we understand the basic concept of the game loop, let's see how to implement it using **Pygame**.

A simple game loop in Pygame looks like this:

```python
python

import pygame
import sys

# Initialize Pygame
pygame.init()

# Set up the game window
screen = pygame.display.set_mode((800, 600))
pygame.display.set_caption("Game Loop Example")

# Set up the game clock
clock = pygame.time.Clock()

# Game variables
player_x = 400
player_y = 300
player_speed = 5

# Main game loop
running = True
```

```python
while running:
    # Event handling
    for event in pygame.event.get():
        if event.type == pygame.QUIT:
            running = False


    # Game updates
    keys = pygame.key.get_pressed()   # Get the
state of all keys
    if keys[pygame.K_LEFT]:
        player_x -= player_speed
    if keys[pygame.K_RIGHT]:
        player_x += player_speed


    # Rendering the scene
    screen.fill((0, 0, 0))   # Fill the screen
with black
    pygame.draw.rect(screen,    (255,    0,    0),
(player_x, player_y, 50, 50))   # Draw the player
    pygame.display.update()   # Update the screen


    # Frame rate control (60 FPS)
    clock.tick(60)

# Quit Pygame
pygame.quit()
sys.exit()
```

Here's how the loop works:

- **Event Handling**: We check for the `QUIT` event (when the window is closed) and listen for key presses (left and right arrow keys to move the player).

- **Game Updates**: Based on key presses, the player's position (`player_x`) is updated.

- **Rendering the Scene**: We fill the screen with a black color, draw the player as a red rectangle, and update the display.

- **Frame Rate Control**: The `clock.tick(60)` line ensures the game runs at 60 frames per second (FPS), giving smooth gameplay.

Optimizing the Loop for Smooth Gameplay (Frame Rate Control)

To ensure smooth gameplay, it's crucial to control the **frame rate** of the game loop. If the frame rate is too low, the game may feel choppy. If it's too high, the game might run too fast or cause unnecessary CPU usage.

Pygame provides the `pygame.time.Clock()` class to help manage the frame rate. The `tick()` method is used to limit the number of frames per second, ensuring the game runs at a consistent speed.

- **Frame Rate**: The **frame rate** (measured in frames per second or FPS) determines how many frames are displayed in one second. A higher FPS results in smoother animations and more responsive controls.

To set a specific frame rate, use `clock.tick(FPS)`, where FPS is the number of frames you want per second. A common frame rate target is **60 FPS**, which is smooth for most games.

Example:

```python

clock.tick(60)   # Limits the game to 60 frames per second
```

This line of code ensures that your game runs at 60 FPS, which is generally fast enough to provide a smooth and responsive experience without overloading the CPU.

- **Delta Time**: For more advanced games, especially those with different hardware, you might need to account for varying frame rates. To ensure consistent movement, developers use **delta time**, which is the time passed between each frame. This helps adjust movement speeds regardless of the frame rate.

Example:

```python
```

```
delta_time = clock.tick(60) / 1000   # Time per
frame in seconds
player_x += player_speed * delta_time   # Adjust
movement based on delta time
```

Conclusion

In this chapter, we explored the concept of the **game loop**, which is central to any game. We learned how the loop handles **events**, **game updates**, and **rendering** to create a dynamic, interactive experience. We also discussed how to **implement the game loop** in Python using Pygame and optimized it for smooth gameplay by controlling the **frame rate**.

With a solid understanding of how the game loop works, you can now build more responsive and interactive games. In the next chapters, we'll dive into creating more advanced game mechanics, like player movement, collision detection, and adding different game elements.

CHAPTER 5

CREATING YOUR FIRST GAME: SETTING UP THE BASICS

In this chapter, we will walk through the process of **creating your first 2D game**. You'll learn how to **plan** and **design** your game, set up the **game window**, and start drawing **basic shapes** like the player, obstacles, and background. Additionally, we will introduce you to **sprites** and **sprite groups**, which are essential for handling game objects efficiently. By the end of this chapter, you'll have the basics set up for your first game, ready to add more complexity in future chapters.

Planning and Designing Your First 2D Game

Before diving into coding, it's important to take some time to plan and design your game. This step ensures that you have a clear vision of what you want to build and helps guide your development process.

Here are some key aspects to consider when planning your first game:

1. **Game**   **Concept**:
   What type of game do you want to create? For your first game, it's a good idea to start with a simple concept. Consider a basic **platformer**, **shooter**, or **endless runner** as a starting point. The goal is to keep it simple while learning the fundamental concepts of game development.

   o For example, in a **platformer**, your player might run and jump across platforms, avoiding obstacles and collecting items.

2. **Game**   **Mechanics**:
   Define how the game will work. Will the player move left and right using the arrow keys? Will there be enemies to avoid or shoot? Decide on basic mechanics like movement, actions, and scoring.

   o For our example, let's say the player controls a simple character that moves left and right and must avoid obstacles while collecting points.

3. **Art**   **and**   **Design**:
   Think about the visual style of the game. Will it be simple and cartoony, or more realistic? For your first game, you can keep the design simple with basic shapes and colors before moving to more complex graphics.

   o Plan the background (e.g., a scrolling landscape), the player's appearance (e.g., a square or circle), and any obstacles (e.g., rectangles or circles).

4. **User** **Interface**:
Think about what the player will see besides the game itself. This might include a **scoreboard**, **health bar**, or **menu screens**. These elements can be kept simple for your first game.

Setting Up the Game Window, Title, and Background

Let's start by setting up the **game window** and **background**.

1. **Create** **the** **Game** **Window**:
The first step in creating a game is to initialize the window where your game will be displayed. This is done using Pygame's `pygame.display.set_mode()` function. It's a good idea to choose a size that will fit comfortably on most screens (e.g., 800x600 pixels).

Example:

```python

import pygame
import sys

# Initialize Pygame
pygame.init()
```

```
# Set up the game window
screen  =  pygame.display.set_mode((800,
600))  # 800x600 pixels
pygame.display.set_caption("My        First
Game")  # Set the window title
```

2. **Setting a Background Color**: You can fill the screen with a solid color using `screen.fill()`. Let's fill the background with a light blue color.

Example:

```
python
```

```
screen.fill((135, 206, 235))  # Fill the
screen with sky blue color
```

Alternatively, you can use an **image** as a background if you have one prepared (e.g., a forest or cityscape). To do this, use the `pygame.image.load()` function to load the image, and `blit()` to draw it to the screen.

Example:

```
python
```

```
background                              =
pygame.image.load("background.png")
```

```
screen.blit(background, (0, 0))  # Draw the
background image at position (0, 0)
```

Drawing Basic Shapes (e.g., Player, Obstacles, Background)

Now that we have the window and background set up, let's start drawing basic shapes for the **player** and **obstacles**.

1. **Drawing   the   Player**:
   To represent the player, we'll use a simple rectangle. You can use the `pygame.draw.rect()` function to draw a rectangle for the player.

   Example:

   python

   ```
   player_width = 50
   player_height = 50
   player_x = 375  # Starting x position
   player_y = 500  # Starting y position
   player_color = (255, 0, 0)  # Red color

   pygame.draw.rect(screen,     player_color,
   (player_x,        player_y,        player_width,
   player_height))
   ```

This will create a red rectangle representing the player, positioned near the bottom center of the screen.

2. **Drawing**   **Obstacles**:

For obstacles, we can draw another rectangle. The player must avoid these obstacles as they move.

Example:

```python

obstacle_width = 50
obstacle_height = 50
obstacle_x = 200  # Starting x position of
the obstacle
obstacle_y = 450  # Starting y position of
the obstacle
obstacle_color = (0, 255, 0)  # Green color

pygame.draw.rect(screen,   obstacle_color,
(obstacle_x,  obstacle_y,  obstacle_width,
obstacle_height))
```

This will create a green rectangle positioned slightly above the player's character, representing an obstacle.

Introduction to Sprites and Sprite Groups

As the game becomes more complex, using basic shapes for all game elements can become cumbersome. This is where **sprites** and **sprite groups** come in. A **sprite** is an object that represents a character or item in a game (e.g., the player, an enemy, a coin). Pygame provides a `Sprite` class to manage these objects efficiently.

1. **Creating   a   Sprite**:
   Let's create a basic player sprite using Pygame's `pygame.sprite.Sprite` class.

   Example:

   ```python
   python

   class Player(pygame.sprite.Sprite):
       def __init__(self):
           super().__init__()
           self.image = pygame.Surface((50,
   50))  # Create a surface for the sprite
           self.image.fill((255, 0, 0))  #
   Fill the sprite with red
           self.rect = self.image.get_rect()
   # Get the rectangle for positioning
           self.rect.x = 375 # Set x position
           self.rect.y = 500 # Set y position
   ```

52

```
def update(self):
        # You can add movement logic here
later
        pass
```

This creates a **Player** sprite that is a red square. The update() method will later be used to handle things like movement or interactions.

2. **Creating a Sprite Group**: A **sprite group** is a container that holds multiple sprites. It allows you to update and draw all the sprites at once. You can add sprites to a group using pygame.sprite.Group().

Example:

python

```
all_sprites = pygame.sprite.Group()    #
Create a group for all sprites
player = Player()  # Create a player object
all_sprites.add(player)    # Add the player
to the sprite group
```

To update and draw all sprites in the group, you can use the following code in the game loop:

python

53

```
all_sprites.update()   # Update all sprites
all_sprites.draw(screen)      #   Draw   all
sprites on the screen
```

Conclusion

In this chapter, you've learned how to create the **basic setup** for your first 2D game. We covered how to **plan and design** your game, how to set up the **game window**, and how to draw **basic shapes** like the player and obstacles. You also got an introduction to **sprites** and **sprite groups**, which will help you manage game objects efficiently as your game grows more complex.

With these foundational elements in place, you're now ready to add more features, like **player movement, collision detection**, and **scoring** in the upcoming chapters. Keep experimenting with the basic shapes and sprites as you continue to build out your game!

CHAPTER 6

HANDLING USER INPUT

In this chapter, we'll explore how to capture and handle **user input**, such as keyboard and mouse actions. We'll focus on moving the player character using the **arrow keys** and **WASD keys**, implementing basic controls like **jumping**, **running**, and **shooting**, and detecting **collisions** between the player and the environment. These are essential elements for making your game interactive and engaging.

Capturing Keyboard and Mouse Input

The first step in handling user input is **capturing** it. In Pygame, you can capture keyboard and mouse input through events or by directly checking the state of the keys or mouse buttons during the game loop.

1. **Keyboard Input (Event Handling)**: The most common way to capture keyboard input is by checking for **key events** during the game loop. Pygame listens for **keydown** (when a key is pressed) and **keyup** (when a key is released) events.

   Example of **event-based input**:

55

python

```
for event in pygame.event.get():
    if event.type == pygame.KEYDOWN:
        if event.key == pygame.K_LEFT:
            player_x -= 5   # Move the
player to the left when the left arrow key
is pressed
        elif event.key == pygame.K_RIGHT:
            player_x += 5   # Move the
player to the right when the right arrow
key is pressed
```

2. **Keyboard Input (Key State Checking)**: Instead of capturing events, you can check the state of the keys using `pygame.key.get_pressed()`. This method returns a list where each index corresponds to a key, and it indicates whether that key is currently pressed.

   Example of **key state checking**:

   python

```
keys = pygame.key.get_pressed()   # Get the
state of all keys
if keys[pygame.K_LEFT]:
    player_x -= 5 # Move the player to the
left when the left arrow key is held down
if keys[pygame.K_RIGHT]:
```

```
player_x += 5  # Move the player to the
right when the right arrow key is held down
```

3. **Mouse** **Input**:

   You can also capture mouse events, such as clicking or moving the mouse, by checking `pygame.MOUSEBUTTONDOWN` (mouse click) or `pygame.MOUSEMOTION` (mouse movement) events.

   Example of **mouse input**:

   python

   ```
   for event in pygame.event.get():
       if          event.type          ==
   pygame.MOUSEBUTTONDOWN:
           if event.button == 1:  # Left mouse
   button
               mouse_x, mouse_y = event.pos  #
   Get the mouse position
               print(f"Mouse     clicked     at
   {mouse_x}, {mouse_y}")
   ```

Creating Basic Character Movement (Arrow Keys, WASD Keys)

Now that we know how to capture keyboard input, let's create basic **character movement** using the arrow keys or WASD keys.

1. **Movement with Arrow Keys**: You can use the arrow keys to move the player left, right, up, and down by modifying the player's position on the screen (represented by a rectangle or sprite).

   Example for **left-right movement** with the arrow keys:

   python

   ```
   keys = pygame.key.get_pressed()  # Get the
   state of all keys
   if keys[pygame.K_LEFT]:
       player_rect.x -= 5  # Move the player
   to the left
   if keys[pygame.K_RIGHT]:
       player_rect.x += 5  # Move the player
   to the right
   ```

2. **Movement with WASD Keys**: Alternatively, you can use the **WASD** keys to control movement. For example, **W** could move the player up, **A** could move left, **S** could move down, and **D** could move right.

   Example for **WASD movement**:

   python

   ```
   if keys[pygame.K_w]:  # W key for moving up
   ```

58

```
    player_rect.y -= 5
if keys[pygame.K_s]:   # S key for moving
down
    player_rect.y += 5
if keys[pygame.K_a]:   # A key for moving
left
    player_rect.x -= 5
if keys[pygame.K_d]:   # D key for moving
right
    player_rect.x += 5
```

Implementing Simple Controls: Jump, Run, Shoot

To make the game more interactive, we need to add controls for actions like **jumping**, **running**, and **shooting**.

1. **Jumping**:

   To implement jumping, you can simulate physics by applying gravity and detecting when the player presses the **spacebar** (or another key) to initiate the jump.

   Example of **jumping**:

   ```python
   gravity = 0.5
   jump_speed = -10
   is_jumping = False
   ```

```
player_y_velocity = 0   # Player's vertical
velocity

if not is_jumping:
    if keys[pygame.K_SPACE]:  # Spacebar to
jump
        player_y_velocity = jump_speed
        is_jumping = True

# Apply gravity
player_y_velocity += gravity
player_rect.y += player_y_velocity

# Prevent the player from falling through
the ground
if player_rect.y >= ground_level:
    player_rect.y = ground_level
    is_jumping = False
    player_y_velocity = 0
```

This basic jump logic adds gravity, a jump speed, and checks if the player has landed on the ground.

2. **Running**:

To implement **running**, you can make the player move faster when a specific key (like **Shift**) is held down.

Example of **running**:

python

```
if keys[pygame.K_LSHIFT]:  # Hold Shift to
run
    player_speed = 10  # Run faster
else:
    player_speed = 5   # Normal walking
speed
```

3. **Shooting**:

For **shooting**, you can spawn bullets or projectiles when the player presses the **spacebar** or **mouse click**. Each projectile moves in a straight line and can interact with enemies or obstacles.

Example of **shooting**:

python

```
if keys[pygame.K_SPACE]:   # Spacebar to
shoot
    bullet  =  Bullet(player_rect.x  +
player_rect.width,    player_rect.y   +
player_rect.height // 2)
    all_sprites.add(bullet)
```

In this example, a **Bullet** object is created every time the spacebar is pressed. The bullet is positioned at the player's current location and added to the sprite group.

61

Detecting Collisions Between the Player and Environment

Detecting **collisions** is crucial in most games, as it allows the player to interact with the environment (e.g., hitting obstacles, collecting items, or being hit by enemies). Pygame provides several ways to check if objects intersect using **rectangles** (bounding boxes).

1. **Collision** **Detection**:
   You can check for collisions between the player and obstacles using Pygame's `pygame.Rect.colliderect()` method, which returns `True` if two rectangles intersect.

   Example for **collision detection**:

   ```python
   python

   if player_rect.colliderect(obstacle_rect):
   # Check if the player hits an obstacle
       print("Player    collided    with    an
   obstacle!")
       # Handle  collision  (e.g.,  decrease
   player health, stop movement, etc.)
   ```

2. **Handling** **Collision** **Effects**:
   Once a collision is detected, you can decide what should

happen. For example, if the player collides with an enemy or obstacle, you might reduce the player's health or restart the level.

Example of **health reduction** after collision:

python

```
if player_rect.colliderect(enemy_rect):
    player_health -= 1  # Reduce health by
1 if the player collides with an enemy
    if player_health <= 0:
        print("Game Over!")
        # Restart or end the game
```

3. **Handling Multiple Collisions**: If you have multiple obstacles or enemies, you can loop through each one and check for collisions with the player.

Example of checking **multiple collisions**:

python

```
for enemy in enemy_group:
    if
player_rect.colliderect(enemy.rect):
        player_health -= 1  # Reduce health
for each collision
```

```
enemy.kill()   # Remove the enemy if
collided
```

Conclusion

In this chapter, we've covered the essential techniques for handling **user input** in your game, including **keyboard** and **mouse** controls. You've learned how to implement basic character **movement**, create **jumping** and **running** actions, and add simple **shooting** mechanics. We also explored how to **detect collisions** between the player and the environment, which is key to creating interactive gameplay.

These fundamental concepts will be the foundation for your game's mechanics. In the next chapters, we'll build on this by adding more complexity, such as enemy AI, levels, and power-ups, to make the game more exciting and engaging!

CHAPTER 7

WORKING WITH IMAGES AND ASSETS

In this chapter, we will learn how to work with images and assets in Pygame. You'll discover how to **import and display images** for elements like **sprites** and **backgrounds**, how to **create custom assets**, understand various **image formats**, and use **sprite animation** to bring your characters and objects to life. Images and assets are the core visual elements of any game, and mastering them will help you create a visually engaging experience.

Importing and Displaying Images (e.g., Sprites, Backgrounds)

Pygame makes it easy to import and display images on the screen. You can use images for everything from **backgrounds** to **sprites** (characters, enemies, items, etc.). The `pygame.image.load()` function is used to load an image file into Pygame, and `blit()` is used to draw it on the screen.

1. **Importing an Image**:
   To use an image in your game, simply load it with `pygame.image.load()`. This function takes the file

path of the image as an argument and returns a surface representing the image.

Example:

```python
```

```
player_image                              =
pygame.image.load('player.png')    # Load
the player sprite
```

2. **Displaying an Image**:
   To display the loaded image on the screen, use the `blit()` method. This method draws the image surface onto the screen surface at a specified position.

   Example:

```python
```

```
screen.blit(player_image,        (player_x,
player_y))   # Draw the player sprite at
position (player_x, player_y)
pygame.display.update()    # Update the
screen to display the image
```

3. **Setting a Background Image**:
   You can also use images for the **background** of your

game. Instead of filling the screen with a color, you can load and display a background image.

Example:

python

```
background_image                      =
pygame.image.load('background.jpg')       #
Load the background image
screen.blit(background_image, (0, 0))    #
Draw the background image at the top-left
corner
pygame.display.update()    # Update the
screen
```

Creating Custom Images and Assets for Your Game

While importing pre-made images can be great, creating your own **custom images and assets** gives your game a unique look. Pygame allows you to create simple graphics on the fly using its **Surface** class. You can draw shapes, add text, and combine them to make assets like buttons, icons, or simple characters.

1. **Creating a Custom Surface**:
   You can create a custom surface (which is essentially a blank canvas) with `pygame.Surface()`. This allows you to draw shapes, fill the surface with colors, and more.

Example:

python

```
custom_surface = pygame.Surface((50, 50))
# Create a 50x50 surface
custom_surface.fill((255, 0, 0))   # Fill
the surface with red color
screen.blit(custom_surface, (100, 100))   #
Draw the surface at position (100, 100)
```

2. **Creating   Custom   Sprites**:
If you want to create a simple sprite, such as a circle or square, you can use Pygame's drawing functions (like `pygame.draw.rect()` or `pygame.draw.circle()`) to add shapes to a surface.

Example of **creating a custom square sprite**:

python

```
square_surface = pygame.Surface((50, 50))
# Create a 50x50 surface
pygame.draw.rect(square_surface, (0, 255,
0), (0, 0, 50, 50))  # Draw a green square
screen.blit(square_surface, (200, 200))   #
Draw the square at (200, 200)
pygame.display.update()     # Update   the
screen
```

3. **Text**   **as**   **Assets**:
Pygame allows you to render text as an image, which can be used for things like labels, scores, or messages. The `pygame.font.Font()` class is used to load a font, and `font.render()` is used to create an image from the text.

Example of **creating a text sprite**:

python

```
font = pygame.font.Font(None, 36)   # Load
a font with size 36
text = font.render("Score: 100", True,
(255, 255, 255))  # Render the text (white
color)
screen.blit(text, (10, 10))   # Draw the
text at position (10, 10)
pygame.display.update()   # Update the
screen
```

Understanding Image Formats (PNG, JPG, GIF, etc.)

When working with images in games, it's important to understand different **image formats**. Different formats are used based on their strengths and weaknesses, depending on the need for transparency, compression, and quality.

1. **PNG (Portable Network Graphics)**: PNG is one of the most commonly used image formats in game development. It supports **transparency** (alpha channel), which is useful for sprites and images that need to be layered over backgrounds. PNG images are **lossless**, meaning they retain the original quality.

   Example of using a PNG image:

   ```python

   sprite = pygame.image.load('sprite.png')
   # PNG images are often used for sprites
   ```

2. **JPG (JPEG)**: JPG is used for high-quality images that need to be compressed, such as backgrounds or large images. However, **JPG images do not support transparency**, and they are **lossy**, meaning some image quality is lost when saving them.

   Example of using a JPG image:

   ```python

   background = pygame.image.load('background.jpg')  # JPG is ideal for backgrounds with no transparency
   ```

3. **GIF (Graphics Interchange Format)**: GIF is commonly used for simple animations and small image files. However, it supports only **256 colors** and doesn't offer the high quality of PNG or JPG. GIF images can have a **transparent background** but don't support complex color gradients.

Example of using a GIF image:

```python
gif_image = pygame.image.load('animation.gif')  # GIFs can be used for simple animations
```

4. **BMP (Bitmap)**: BMP is an uncompressed format that is rarely used in game development due to its large file size. However, it supports basic color images without compression artifacts.

Example of using a BMP image:

```python
bmp_image = pygame.image.load('image.bmp')
# BMP can be used but isn't efficient for large assets
```

71

Tip: For most games, **PNG** is the best choice for images that require transparency (like sprites), and **JPG** is ideal for static background images that don't need transparency.

Animating Sprites with Frames of Animation

In many games, characters and objects need to **animate** to create a dynamic and lively experience. You can animate a sprite by cycling through multiple **frames** of an image, each showing a different part of the animation.

1. **Using   a   Sprite   Sheet**:
   A **sprite sheet** is a single image file that contains multiple frames of an animation arranged in a grid. You can extract each frame from the sheet and display them sequentially to create the animation.

   Example of **loading and animating a sprite from a sprite sheet**:

   ```python
   sprite_sheet                                    =
   pygame.image.load('spritesheet.png')        #
   Load the sprite sheet

   # Assume each frame is 50x50 pixels
   ```

```python
frame_width = 50
frame_height = 50

# Extract the frames from the sprite sheet
walking_frames = []
for i in range(4):  # Assume there are 4
frames in the sprite sheet
    frame = sprite_sheet.subsurface(i *
frame_width, 0, frame_width, frame_height)
    walking_frames.append(frame)

# Display the current frame
current_frame = walking_frames[0]  # Get
the first frame
screen.blit(current_frame,      (player_x,
player_y))
```

2. **Animating   with   Frame   Switching**:
To animate the sprite, you can cycle through the frames at
regular intervals. You can use a counter to switch between
frames, creating the illusion of movement.

Example of **animating the player sprite**:

python

```python
frame_count = 0
current_frame = walking_frames[frame_count
// 10]  # Change frame every 10 iterations
```

73

```
frame_count += 1
if frame_count >= 40:  # Reset the counter
after 40 frames
    frame_count = 0

# Draw the current frame
screen.blit(current_frame,       (player_x,
player_y))
```

This will display the animation and cycle through the frames based on the frame counter.

3. **Smooth**   **Animation**:
To make the animation smoother, you can control the frame rate and the timing between each frame. Instead of switching frames every 10 iterations, you can adjust this interval to fine-tune the animation speed.

Example of **smoother frame switching**:

```python
frame_rate = 5   # Frame rate controls the
speed of the animation
if frame_count % frame_rate == 0:
    current_frame                            =
walking_frames[(frame_count // frame_rate)
% len(walking_frames)]
```

74

Conclusion

In this chapter, we explored how to **import and display images** in your game, how to **create custom assets** using Pygame's `Surface` class, and how to work with different **image formats** like PNG, JPG, GIF, and BMP. We also introduced the concept of **sprite animation** and how to animate sprites using **sprite sheets** and frame cycling.

Mastering images and assets will allow you to bring your game to life visually. In the next chapters, we'll build on this foundation by adding more complex game mechanics, such as **player movement**, **collisions**, and **game levels**. Keep experimenting with images, animations, and custom assets to give your game its unique look and feel!

CHAPTER 8

ADDING SOUND AND MUSIC TO YOUR GAME

In this chapter, we will explore how to **add sound effects** and **background music** to your game, enhancing the overall player experience. We will cover the basics of working with audio in Python, using Pygame's `pygame.mixer` module. You will also learn about **audio formats**, how to implement sound effects (e.g., collision sounds, jump sounds), and how to manage the volume and looping of sounds.

Understanding Audio Formats and Libraries in Python

When working with audio in games, it's important to understand the different **audio formats** that can be used and which ones are best suited for various types of sound.

1. **Common Audio Formats**:
    o **WAV**: WAV files are **uncompressed** audio files, meaning they are high-quality but tend to be large in file size. They are commonly used for short sound effects, like jumps, explosions, or collisions.

76

- o **MP3**: MP3 files are **compressed**, meaning they are smaller in size but sacrifice some quality. They are ideal for background music because they allow longer tracks without taking up too much space.
- o **OGG**: OGG is a compressed format similar to MP3 but with **better compression** and **higher quality**. It's often used for both sound effects and background music in games.

2. **Pygame's Audio Library**: Pygame's `pygame.mixer` module is used to manage sounds and music. It supports **WAV, MP3, OGG**, and **MIDI** formats for sound effects and background music.

To use Pygame's mixer, you first need to initialize it:

```python
python
```

```python
import pygame
pygame.mixer.init()  # Initialize the mixer
for sound handling
```

Once initialized, you can use `pygame.mixer.Sound()` for sound effects and `pygame.mixer.music` for background music.

Implementing Sound Effects (e.g., Collision, Jump Sounds)

One of the most important aspects of sound in games is **sound effects**. Sound effects add depth and feedback to the gameplay, enhancing the player's emotional response. Common sound effects in games include sounds for **collisions**, **jumps**, **shooting**, and **level-ups**.

1. **Loading and Playing Sound Effects**: You can load a sound file into Pygame using `pygame.mixer.Sound()`. Once loaded, you can play it using `.play()`.

   Example of **playing a jump sound**:

   ```python
   jump_sound                            =
   pygame.mixer.Sound("jump.wav")  # Load the
   jump sound
   jump_sound.play()  # Play the jump sound
   ```

2. **Sound Effects on Events**: You can trigger sound effects in response to in-game events, such as a collision between the player and an obstacle, or the player jumping.

   Example of **collision sound**:

   ```python
   ```

```
collision_sound                          =
pygame.mixer.Sound("collision.wav")      #
Load the collision sound

if player_rect.colliderect(obstacle_rect):
# Check if the player collides with an
obstacle
    collision_sound.play()    # Play the
collision sound
```

This will play the collision sound every time the player collides with an obstacle.

Adding Background Music to Your Game

Background music plays a significant role in setting the tone of your game. Whether it's energetic, peaceful, or suspenseful, the right background music enhances the emotional experience.

1. **Loading and Playing Background Music**: Pygame's `pygame.mixer.music` module is used for playing background music. Unlike sound effects, background music is typically a long audio file that loops or plays continuously throughout the game.

    To load and play background music:

    ```python
    python
    ```

```
pygame.mixer.music.load("background_music
.mp3")  # Load the background music
pygame.mixer.music.play(-1, 0.0)  # Play
the music on loop (-1 means infinite loop)
```

2. **Controlling Music Playback**: You can control the background music in several ways, including pausing, stopping, and adjusting the volume.

   o **Pausing and Resuming**:

   python

   ```
   pygame.mixer.music.pause()  # Pause
   the music
   pygame.mixer.music.unpause()      #
   Resume the music
   ```

   o **Stopping Music**:

   python

   ```
   pygame.mixer.music.stop()  # Stop
   the music
   ```

   o **Changing the Volume**: You can set the volume of the music or sound effects using the .set_volume() method. The volume is set between 0.0 (silent) and 1.0 (full volume).

80

Example of adjusting the volume:

```python
python
```

```python
pygame.mixer.music.set_volume(0.5)
# Set background music volume to 50%
```

Similarly, you can control the volume of sound effects:

```python
python
```

```python
jump_sound.set_volume(0.8)    # Set
the jump sound volume to 80%
```

Controlling Sound Volume and Looping

In addition to controlling playback, you often want to adjust the **volume** of your sounds and **looping**. Pygame provides simple functions to manage both.

1. **Sound Volume Control**: You can control the volume of both background music and sound effects. This is useful for balancing the sound levels between different elements of your game.

   Example of adjusting **sound effect volume**:

```python
python
```

81

```
collision_sound.set_volume(0.3)      # Set
collision sound volume to 30%
```

Example of adjusting **background music volume**:

```
python
```

```
pygame.mixer.music.set_volume(0.6)   # Set
music volume to 60%
```

2. **Looping Sound Effects**: For some sound effects, such as a looping ambient noise or music, you might want to play them in a loop. Pygame's `play()` method supports the `loops` argument, which controls how many times the sound repeats.

   Example of looping a sound:

```
python
```

```
background_ambience              =
pygame.mixer.Sound("ambient_noise.wav")
background_ambience.play(loops=-1,
maxtime=0)    # Loop indefinitely (until
manually stopped)
```

3. **Looping Background Music**: For background music, Pygame automatically loops the music if you specify -1

in the `play()` function, as shown earlier. You can also stop the music when the game is over, or when transitioning between scenes.

Conclusion

In this chapter, we covered how to **add sound effects** and **background music** to your game, which are essential for creating an immersive and engaging player experience. You learned how to import and play sound files using Pygame's `pygame.mixer` module, implement common sound effects (such as **jump** and **collision sounds**), and add **background music** that plays throughout the game. Additionally, you explored how to control the **volume** of sounds and manage **looping** to maintain a continuous and enjoyable audio experience.

Sound adds depth to the game and helps convey emotions, so experimenting with different sound effects and music can significantly enhance your game. In the following chapters, we will continue building upon the game mechanics and explore more advanced topics like **AI**, **collision detection**, and **game progression**.

CHAPTER 9

BUILDING A SIMPLE GAME: THE PLAYER AND ENEMIES

In this chapter, we will build a simple **player vs. enemy** game scenario. You will learn how to create player movement and actions (such as jumping and attacking), set up enemy behavior (including movement and collision detection), and manage the dynamic spawning and despawning of enemies. This is where we'll start bringing together all the concepts we've learned so far, such as handling user input, animation, and collision detection, to create an interactive game.

Designing Your First Basic Game: A Player vs. Enemy Scenario

Before diving into the code, let's design a simple game concept. In this game, the player controls a character who must avoid or defeat enemies. The basic setup will be a platformer-style game where the player can move left and right, jump, and attack. The enemies will move toward the player and, when colliding, cause the player to lose health or restart the game.

Here's what we need to build:

1. **Player** **Character**:

   The player can move left, right, and jump. The character can also attack enemies by pressing a key.

2. **Enemies**:

   The enemies will move toward the player, and when they collide with the player, the player loses health.

3. **Goal**:

   The player must avoid or defeat the enemies to survive. For simplicity, the goal is to last as long as possible.

Creating Player Movement and Actions (Jumping, Attacking)

To begin, let's implement basic **player movement**. We'll use the **arrow keys** or **WASD keys** for movement, and **spacebar** for jumping. We'll also create an **attack** mechanic that lets the player shoot at enemies using a separate key (e.g., **Z**).

1. **Player** **Movement**:

   The player should be able to move left and right and jump. We'll use the `pygame.key.get_pressed()` function to detect the movement keys.

   Example of **player movement**:

   python

   ```python
   player_speed = 5
   ```

85

```
player_x, player_y = 100, 500  # Starting
position
player_velocity_y = 0
is_jumping = False


# Movement with WASD keys or Arrow keys
keys = pygame.key.get_pressed()
if          keys[pygame.K_LEFT]          or
keys[pygame.K_a]:  # Move left
    player_x -= player_speed
if          keys[pygame.K_RIGHT]         or
keys[pygame.K_d]:  # Move right
    player_x += player_speed
```

2. **Jumping**:

We'll simulate jumping by applying gravity to the player's vertical movement. The player can jump by pressing the **spacebar**. Once the player presses the spacebar, we'll set the vertical velocity (player_velocity_y) to a negative value, which will simulate the upward force of the jump.

Example of **jumping**:

```
python


gravity = 0.5
jump_speed = -10
if not is_jumping:
```

86

```
    if keys[pygame.K_SPACE]:  # Jump with
spacebar
        player_velocity_y = jump_speed
        is_jumping = True


# Apply gravity
player_velocity_y += gravity
player_y += player_velocity_y


# Prevent the player from falling through
the ground
if player_y >= 500:  # Ground level
    player_y = 500
    is_jumping = False
    player_velocity_y = 0
```

3. **Attacking**:

For simplicity, let's implement a **shooting** mechanic where pressing the **Z key** will create a bullet that moves across the screen. We'll use a `Bullet` class to handle the bullet object.

Example of **shooting**:

python

```
class Bullet(pygame.sprite.Sprite):
    def __init__(self, x, y):
        super().__init__()
```

87

```
        self.image  =  pygame.Surface((10,
5))  # Bullet size
        self.image.fill((255, 0, 0))  # Red
bullet
        self.rect = self.image.get_rect()
        self.rect.x = x
        self.rect.y = y


    def update(self):
        self.rect.x  +=  10    #  Move  the
bullet to the right


bullets = pygame.sprite.Group()


if keys[pygame.K_z]:  # Shoot with Z key
    bullet = Bullet(player_x + 50, player_y
+ 25)
    bullets.add(bullet)


# Update and draw bullets
bullets.update()
bullets.draw(screen)
```

Setting Up Enemy Behavior (Movement, Collision Detection)

Enemies need to move toward the player and detect collisions. We'll start by making the enemy move towards the player's position. When the enemy collides with the player, we will reduce the player's health or trigger a game-over condition.

1. **Enemy**   **Movement**:

   The enemy will move toward the player by updating its x and y coordinates. For simplicity, we'll make the enemy **follow** the player along the x-axis.

   Example of **enemy movement**:

   python

```python
class Enemy(pygame.sprite.Sprite):
    def __init__(self, x, y):
        super().__init__()
        self.image = pygame.Surface((50,
50))  # Enemy size
        self.image.fill((0, 255, 0))   #
Green enemy
        self.rect = self.image.get_rect()
        self.rect.x = x
        self.rect.y = y
        self.speed = 2

    def update(self):
        if self.rect.x < player_x:  # Move
right
            self.rect.x += self.speed
```

```
        elif self.rect.x > player_x:    #
Move left
            self.rect.x -= self.speed

enemy = Enemy(600, 500)
enemies = pygame.sprite.Group()
enemies.add(enemy)

# Update and draw enemies
enemies.update()
enemies.draw(screen)
```

2. **Collision** **Detection**:

We'll check if the player's rectangle (player_rect) collides with any enemy's rectangle (enemy.rect). If they collide, the player's health will decrease.

Example of **collision detection**:

python

```
if player_rect.colliderect(enemy.rect):    #
If the player collides with an enemy
    player_health -= 1   # Decrease health
by 1
    enemy.kill()   # Remove the enemy
```

Spawning and Despawning Enemies Dynamically

For a dynamic experience, we can spawn enemies at random positions and despawn them when they are defeated or move off-screen. We can also spawn new enemies after a certain time or when the player reaches a specific milestone.

1. **Spawning**   **Enemies**:

    We'll spawn enemies at random intervals by adding new Enemy objects to the game. These enemies will be added to the enemies group.

    Example of **enemy spawning**:

    python

```python
import random

def spawn_enemy():
    enemy_x = random.randint(50, 750)   # Random x position
    enemy_y = random.randint(50, 550)   # Random y position
    enemy = Enemy(enemy_x, enemy_y)
    enemies.add(enemy)

# Spawn an enemy every 2 seconds
if pygame.time.get_ticks() % 2000 < 20:   # Check if 2 seconds have passed
```

91

```
spawn_enemy()
```

2. **Despawning** **Enemies**:

To remove enemies that are defeated or go off-screen, you can use the `kill()` method to remove them from the group.

Example of **despawning enemies**:

```python
python
```

```python
for enemy in enemies:
    if enemy.rect.x < 0 or enemy.rect.x >
800:  # If the enemy moves off-screen
        enemy.kill()  # Remove the enemy
```

Conclusion

In this chapter, you learned how to create a simple **player vs. enemy** game. We covered the basic mechanics of **player movement** (left, right, and jumping), implementing **attacks** (shooting bullets), and creating enemy behavior (movement and collision detection). We also explored how to **spawn** and **despawn** enemies dynamically to keep the game challenging.

With these building blocks, you have the foundation to create a more complex game. In future chapters, we'll enhance this basic setup by adding **scoring**, **levels**, **power-ups**, and more advanced **enemy AI**. Keep experimenting with these concepts to refine your game and make it more engaging!

CHAPTER 11

HANDLING COLLISIONS AND PHYSICS

In this chapter, we will dive into the world of **collisions** and **physics**, two key components of any interactive game. You will learn how to handle different types of **collision detection** (such as rectangles and circles), how to add **simple physics** like gravity, friction, and bouncing, and how to implement smooth character and object interactions. These features will make your game feel more realistic and dynamic.

Introduction to Collision Detection in 2D Games

Collision detection is the process of determining when two or more game objects **intersect** or come into contact with each other. In 2D games, the most common types of collision detection are based on **shapes** such as rectangles, circles, and polygons.

Collision detection is essential for game mechanics such as:

- **Player-Object Interactions**: Detecting when the player hits an obstacle or enemy.

- **Movement and Boundaries**: Ensuring the player doesn't move through walls or floors.
- **Projectile-Enemy Interactions**: Detecting when bullets hit enemies or obstacles.

Pygame provides several ways to handle collisions. The simplest approach uses **rectangles** (bounding boxes) to represent game objects. For more complex interactions, you can also use **circles** or **pixel-perfect collisions**.

Handling Different Types of Collisions: Rectangle, Circle

1. **Rectangle Collision Detection**: The easiest and most commonly used collision detection in 2D games is **rectangle-based** collision detection. Each game object is given a rectangular boundary (using `pygame.Rect`), and the collision is detected by checking if two rectangles intersect.

   Pygame's `pygame.Rect.colliderect()` method is used to detect collisions between two rectangles.

   Example of **rectangle collision**:

   ```python
   python
   ```

```
player_rect    =    pygame.Rect(player_x,
player_y, player_width, player_height)
enemy_rect = pygame.Rect(enemy_x, enemy_y,
enemy_width, enemy_height)

if player_rect.colliderect(enemy_rect):   #
Check if the player collides with the enemy
    print("Collision detected!")
```

This will return `True` if the two rectangles overlap and `False` otherwise.

2. **Circle Collision Detection**: In some cases, using rectangles for collision detection may not be accurate enough, especially when dealing with round objects. For such cases, we can use **circle-based** collision detection.

   Pygame provides `pygame.math.Vector2` and `colliderect()` methods for circle collision, but we often rely on calculating the distance between the centers of two circles and comparing it to their radii.

   Example of **circle collision**:

   python

   ```
   import math
   ```

```
def  check_circle_collision(player_center,
player_radius,              enemy_center,
enemy_radius):
    distance = math.sqrt((player_center[0]
- enemy_center[0])**2 + (player_center[1]
- enemy_center[1])**2)
    if   distance  <  player_radius   +
enemy_radius:
        return True  # Collision detected
    return False
```

This calculates the Euclidean distance between the two circles' centers and checks if the distance is less than the sum of their radii.

Adding Simple Physics: Gravity, Friction, Bouncing

1. **Gravity**: Gravity is one of the most common physics simulations in games. It pulls objects downward at a constant rate, and it's essential for platformers, falling objects, or any game where the player needs to feel the effect of gravity.

   In Pygame, we can simulate gravity by adjusting the **vertical velocity** (y_velocity) of the player. Each time the game loop runs, we add gravity to the vertical velocity, and then update the player's vertical position accordingly.

Example of **gravity**:

python

```
gravity = 0.5  # Gravity force
jump_speed = -10
player_velocity_y = 0
player_rect.y += player_velocity_y  #
Update player position

if not is_jumping:
    player_velocity_y += gravity  # Apply
gravity if not jumping
```

When the player is not jumping, the velocity will keep increasing, simulating gravity pulling the player down. When the player is jumping, gravity will slow the upward motion, eventually pulling the player back down.

2. **Friction**: Friction is the force that resists the motion of an object. In games, we often simulate friction by reducing the player's speed when no input is being given (e.g., the player stops moving after releasing the movement keys).

Example of **friction**:

```python
python

friction = 0.95  # Friction factor (between
0 and 1)
if   not   keys[pygame.K_LEFT]   and   not
keys[pygame.K_RIGHT]:
    player_velocity_x  *=  friction      #
Gradually slow the player down
```

When no movement keys are pressed, the player's velocity will decrease, simulating friction. The player will gradually stop moving.

3. **Bouncing**: To simulate **bouncing**, you can reverse the direction of the velocity when an object hits the ground or another surface. This can be done by multiplying the velocity by a negative value (for vertical motion, when the object hits the ground).

Example of **bouncing**:

```python
python

if player_rect.y >= ground_level:
    player_velocity_y = -player_velocity_y
* 0.8  # Reverse the velocity and apply a
bounce factor
```

The bounce factor (e.g., `0.8`) controls how much energy is lost during the bounce. A value of `1.0` would mean no energy loss, while a lower value would simulate a more realistic, energy-losing bounce.

Implementing Smooth Character and Object Interactions

In addition to basic physics and collision detection, **smooth interactions** between characters and objects are essential to make the game feel more natural. This includes ensuring that the character reacts appropriately to objects, such as standing on platforms or being pushed by forces like wind or explosions.

1. **Character-Object Interaction (Standing on Platforms)**: When a player is standing on a platform, you need to check for **ground collisions** to ensure the player doesn't fall through the platform. This can be done by checking if the player's bottom is touching the top of the platform and preventing them from moving further down.

   Example of **standing on platforms**:

   python

   ```python
   if player_rect.colliderect(platform_rect):
   # If the player touches the platform
   ```

```
    player_rect.y = platform_rect.top -
player_rect.height  # Set player on top of
the platform
    player_velocity_y = 0  # Stop the
downward movement
```

2. **Smooth Movement Across Obstacles**: If the player is moving through a series of obstacles, you'll need to handle **smooth movement** so the player doesn't get stuck on edges. By checking for nearby collisions and adjusting the position of the player, you can make the movement feel more fluid.

   Example of **smooth movement**:

   python

```
player_rect.x += player_velocity_x  # Move
player horizontally
if player_rect.colliderect(obstacle_rect):
# If player collides with obstacle
    player_rect.x -= player_velocity_x  #
Revert the movement
```

3. **Simulating Smooth Interaction with Objects**: For objects like **platforms, obstacles, and collectibles**, we need to ensure smooth interactions. For example, the player can **collect items** (such as coins or power-ups),

which can be done by detecting collisions with the items and then removing them from the game world.

Example of **collecting an item**:

```python

for item in items:
    if player_rect.colliderect(item.rect):
# If the player collects an item
        items.remove(item)    # Remove the
item from the list
        player_score += 10    # Increase
player score
```

Conclusion

In this chapter, we covered the essentials of **collision detection** and **physics** in 2D games. You learned how to handle **rectangle and circle collisions**, simulate **gravity, friction**, and **bouncing**, and implement **smooth interactions** between the player and the environment. These concepts are crucial for creating engaging and realistic game mechanics that respond well to user input and in-game events.

By incorporating these features into your game, you can enhance the player experience, making the game feel more interactive and dynamic. In future chapters, we will continue to refine these mechanics and build upon them with more advanced gameplay elements, such as AI, power-ups, and level progression.

CHAPTER 12

GAME AI: MAKING ENEMIES SMARTER

In this chapter, we will introduce the basics of **game AI** (Artificial Intelligence) and explore how to make your enemies smarter and more challenging. We will cover fundamental concepts like **pathfinding** and **decision-making**, and show you how to implement these ideas in your game using **Pygame**. By the end of this chapter, your enemies will be able to **chase** the player, **patrol** areas, and exhibit **random behavior**, all of which will enhance the challenge and make the game more engaging.

Basics of Game AI: Pathfinding, Decision-Making

1. **Pathfinding**:

   Pathfinding refers to the method by which an AI-controlled character navigates through a game world, finding the shortest or most efficient route from one point to another while avoiding obstacles. Common algorithms for pathfinding in games include *A (A-star)**, **Dijkstra's algorithm**, and **Breadth-First Search**. For simplicity, in this chapter, we will focus on basic **chasing** and **patrolling** behavior rather than implementing complex pathfinding algorithms.

2. **Decision-Making**:

   Decision-making is the process by which the AI decides what action to take based on the environment and its goals. This is usually handled through **state machines**, **decision trees**, or simpler methods like random decisions. For example, an enemy might decide to either **chase** the player or **patrol** the area based on certain conditions, such as the player's position or the enemy's health.

In Pygame, game AI can be implemented by creating simple classes that handle enemy behavior. We'll use basic conditional logic and position checking to make enemies move toward the player or follow a patrol route.

Implementing Basic Enemy AI Using Pygame

Let's start by creating a basic **Enemy** class with simple AI behavior. The AI will allow the enemy to either **chase** the player if they are close or **patrol** a specific area when they are not.

1. **Enemy Class Setup**: The `Enemy` class will have properties for position, speed, and behavior. We'll also define methods for updating the enemy's actions (chasing, patrolling).

Example of **basic Enemy class**:

python

```python
import pygame
import random

class Enemy(pygame.sprite.Sprite):
    def __init__(self, x, y):
        super().__init__()
        self.image = pygame.Surface((50,
50))  # Size of the enemy
        self.image.fill((255, 0, 0))  # Red
color for the enemy
        self.rect = self.image.get_rect()
        self.rect.x = x
        self.rect.y = y
        self.speed = 2
        self.patrol_range = 100  # The area
the enemy patrols
        self.patrol_direction         =
random.choice([-1, 1])   # Random  patrol
direction
        self.chasing = False  # Initially
not chasing the player

    def update(self, player_rect):
        if self.chasing:

self.chase_player(player_rect)
```

```
        else:
            self.patrol()

    def chase_player(self, player_rect):
        """Move toward the player."""
        if self.rect.x < player_rect.x:
            self.rect.x += self.speed    #
Move right
        elif self.rect.x > player_rect.x:
            self.rect.x -= self.speed    #
Move left

        if self.rect.y < player_rect.y:
            self.rect.y += self.speed    #
Move down
        elif self.rect.y > player_rect.y:
            self.rect.y -= self.speed    #
Move up

    def patrol(self):
        """Patrol back and forth within a
specified range."""
        self.rect.x    +=    self.speed    *
self.patrol_direction # Move left or right

        # Reverse patrol direction if the
enemy moves too far in one direction
        if self.rect.x < 0 or self.rect.x
> 800:   # Assuming 800px width screen
```

```
self.patrol_direction *= -1
```

In this code:

- The **Enemy** class inherits from `pygame.sprite.Sprite` to take advantage of sprite management.
- The **update()** method checks if the enemy should be **chasing** the player or **patrolling** a predefined area.
- The **chase_player()** method moves the enemy towards the player's position.
- The **patrol()** method moves the enemy back and forth along the x-axis within a certain range.

Moving Enemies Toward the Player (Chase, Patrol)

To make the enemy **chase** the player, we first check if the enemy is within a certain distance from the player. If the player is close enough, the enemy will start chasing them. If the player is far away, the enemy will return to its patrol route.

Here's how we can implement **chasing** the player:

- We'll check the distance between the player and enemy and trigger the `chase_player()` method when the player is within a specific range.

Example of **chasing behavior**:

python

```
def update_enemy_behavior(self, player_rect):
    distance_to_player                        =
pygame.math.Vector2(player_rect.x - self.rect.x,
player_rect.y - self.rect.y).length()

    if distance_to_player < 200:  # Enemy will
chase if within 200 pixels of the player
        self.chasing = True
    else:
        self.chasing = False
```

This method calculates the **distance** between the player and enemy using **vector math** and checks if the distance is below a threshold (in this case, 200 pixels). If the enemy is within this range, it will **chase** the player; otherwise, it will resume **patrolling**.

Using Random Behavior for More Challenge

To make the enemy behavior more unpredictable and challenging, you can implement **random behavior**. Instead of having enemies always chase or patrol, you can make them **switch between behaviors** randomly, adding variety to the gameplay.

1. **Random** **Behavior**:
Randomizing the enemy's actions can make them less predictable and more challenging to avoid or defeat. We can make the enemy **occasionally** change between patrolling and chasing based on a random chance.

Example of **random behavior**:

python

```
def random_behavior(self):
    if random.random() < 0.01:   # 1% chance to
switch behavior
        self.chasing = not self.chasing  # Toggle
chasing state
```

This function randomly changes the enemy's behavior with a 1% chance every frame. This can make the game feel more dynamic, as enemies might suddenly change their behavior unexpectedly.

Putting It All Together

Here's how we can integrate everything into the game loop:

1. **Create and update enemy objects** in the game loop.
2. **Check for collisions** between the player and enemy, and update the player's health or trigger a game-over condition when needed.

110

3. **Randomize enemy behavior** and toggle between patrolling and chasing to keep the gameplay engaging.

Example of **game loop with enemy AI**:

python

```python
# Game loop
player_rect = pygame.Rect(player_x, player_y,
50, 50)  # Player position
enemies = pygame.sprite.Group()  # Group of
enemies

# Create some enemies
enemy1 = Enemy(100, 100)
enemy2 = Enemy(400, 200)
enemies.add(enemy1, enemy2)

# Update the game
for enemy in enemies:
    enemy.update(player_rect)  # Update enemy
behavior based on player position
    enemy.random_behavior()  # Occasionally
change behavior

    if player_rect.colliderect(enemy.rect):  #
Check for collision with the player
        player_health -= 1 # Decrease health on
collision
```

This loop checks for collisions between the player and enemies and updates their behavior (whether chasing or patrolling). The enemies will randomly switch behaviors, and the player will lose health when colliding with them.

Conclusion

In this chapter, we learned the basics of **game AI**, focusing on **enemy behavior** such as **chasing** the player, **patrolling** a specific area, and implementing **random behavior** to make the enemies more unpredictable. We also created a simple **Enemy class** with AI logic, and incorporated it into the game loop for dynamic interactions between the player and enemies.

AI in games can become as complex as you like, from basic chasing and patrolling to advanced pathfinding and decision-making. In future chapters, we will continue to build on this AI foundation, exploring more advanced behaviors, such as **group tactics**, **intelligent decision-making**, and **dynamic difficulty adjustment** to create a more immersive gaming experience.

CHAPTER 13

BUILDING A SIMPLE PLATFORMER

In this chapter, we will create a **simple 2D platformer** game. Platformers are a popular genre where the player moves across platforms, jumps over obstacles, and avoids falling. You will learn about the core mechanics of platformers, such as **jumping** and **running**, designing a **platformer level**, handling **gravity** and **jumping physics**, and creating **platforms** and **obstacles**. By the end of this chapter, you'll have a basic platformer where the player can navigate through a level by jumping and running across platforms.

Introduction to Platformer Mechanics (Jumping, Running)

Platformers are built around two fundamental mechanics: **jumping** and **running**. These mechanics allow the player to navigate the game world by moving across platforms, jumping over obstacles, and reaching new areas.

1. **Running**:

   In a platformer, running allows the player to move quickly

across the level. The player can move left and right, often controlled by the **arrow keys** or **WASD keys**.

2. **Jumping**:

   Jumping allows the player to reach higher platforms, avoid obstacles, or escape hazards. Jumping is typically controlled by pressing the **spacebar**. It's important to simulate physics so the jump feels natural—meaning it should start with an upward velocity, slow down, and then be affected by gravity.

Designing a Simple 2D Platformer Level

The next step is designing the level itself. A **platformer level** is usually composed of different platforms, obstacles, and a starting/ending point. In a 2D game, the level is typically represented as a grid of tiles or rectangles.

1. **Creating the Level Layout**:

   For simplicity, we can create a basic level where the player can run and jump from platform to platform. The level could consist of platforms arranged at different heights and obstacles scattered across the screen.

   Example of **platforms and obstacles**:

   python

```
platforms = [
    pygame.Rect(100, 500, 200, 20),    #
Platform   at   x=100,   y=500,   width=200,
height=20
    pygame.Rect(400, 400, 200, 20),    #
Platform at x=400, y=400
    pygame.Rect(700, 300, 200, 20)     #
Platform at x=700, y=300
]
```

2. **Creating a Simple Level with Platforms**: We can start by drawing the platforms and obstacles on the screen. Platforms can be represented as rectangles, and the player must jump between them to progress through the level.

   Example of **drawing the level**:

   ```
   python
   ```

   ```
   for platform in platforms:
       pygame.draw.rect(screen, (0, 255, 0),
   platform)  # Draw green platforms
   ```

Handling Gravity and Jumping Physics

In a platformer, **gravity** pulls the player down, and the **jumping physics** make the player move upward before gravity takes over.

We'll implement basic physics for jumping, including applying gravity and detecting when the player is on the ground.

1. **Gravity**:

   Gravity is a force that continuously pulls the player down, simulating a natural falling motion. We'll add gravity to the player's vertical velocity each frame.

   Example of **gravity simulation**:

   python

   ```python
   gravity = 0.5   # The gravity force (how fast the player falls)
   jump_speed = -10   # The initial jump speed (negative to go up)

   # Player's vertical velocity
   player_velocity_y = 0

   # Apply gravity when the player is not jumping
   if not is_jumping:
       player_velocity_y += gravity
   ```

2. **Jumping**:

   When the player presses the **spacebar**, the vertical velocity is set to a negative value (simulating the jump). The player will then move upward and, eventually,

116

gravity will slow the ascent, pull the player back down, and cause the player to land on the platforms.

Example of **jumping physics**:

python

```
if not is_jumping:
    if keys[pygame.K_SPACE]:  # Spacebar to
jump
        player_velocity_y = jump_speed
        is_jumping = True


# Update the player's position based on
vertical velocity
player_rect.y += player_velocity_y


# Prevent the player from falling through
the ground
if player_rect.y >= ground_level:  # If the
player reaches the ground level
    player_rect.y = ground_level
    is_jumping = False
    player_velocity_y = 0  # Reset vertical
velocity
```

3. **Collisions   with   Platforms**:
When the player is falling and lands on a platform, you need to check if the player's **rectangle** collides with the

117

platform. If a collision is detected, the player should stop falling and be placed on top of the platform.

Example of **collision with platforms**:

python

```
for platform in platforms:
    if player_rect.colliderect(platform):
# If player collides with platform
        player_rect.y = platform.top -
player_rect.height  # Place player on top
of platform
        player_velocity_y = 0  # Stop
downward velocity
        is_jumping = False  # The player is
no longer jumping
```

Creating Platforms and Obstacles

In platformer games, obstacles and platforms serve as the core elements of the level design. Let's create platforms that the player can jump on, and obstacles that the player needs to avoid.

1. **Creating   Platforms**:
   Platforms are static rectangles where the player can stand. We can create multiple platforms with varying **x** and **y** positions, as well as different widths.

118

Example of **platform creation**:

python

```
platform1 = pygame.Rect(100, 400, 200, 20)
# A platform at position (100, 400)
platform2 = pygame.Rect(400, 300, 200, 20)
# Another platform at position (400, 300)
```

2. **Drawing   Platforms**:

To visualize the platforms, you can use `pygame.draw.rect()` to draw them as simple shapes on the screen. The platforms will be drawn in the game loop.

Example of **drawing platforms**:

python

```
for platform in platforms:
    pygame.draw.rect(screen, (0, 255, 0),
platform)  # Draw each platform in green
```

3. **Obstacles**:

You can also add obstacles to the level to increase the challenge. These obstacles can be static (like spikes or walls) or dynamic (like moving enemies). For simplicity, let's use rectangles for obstacles.

119

Example of **adding obstacles**:

python

```
obstacle = pygame.Rect(500, 450, 50, 50)  #
Create a rectangular obstacle at position
(500, 450)
```

Example of **drawing obstacles**:

python

```
pygame.draw.rect(screen, (255, 0, 0),
obstacle)  # Draw obstacles in red
```

4. **Collision with Obstacles**:
If the player collides with an obstacle, you can trigger a **game over** or reduce the player's health.

Example of **collision with obstacles**:

python

```
if player_rect.colliderect(obstacle):
    player_health -= 1  # Decrease player
health on collision
    if player_health <= 0:
        game_over()  # Trigger game over
function
```

Conclusion

In this chapter, we learned the fundamental mechanics of **platformers**, including **jumping**, **running**, and handling **gravity**. We also explored how to design a **2D platformer level** with platforms and obstacles, implement **jumping physics**, and create a basic player movement system. You now have a basic platformer where the player can jump from platform to platform and avoid obstacles.

With these core mechanics in place, you can continue expanding the game by adding more complex elements like **moving platforms**, **enemies**, **collectibles**, and **level progression**. The concepts covered here are essential for creating a fun and interactive platformer experience. In the next chapters, we'll dive deeper into adding more features and refining the gameplay.

CHAPTER 14

POWER-UPS AND SPECIAL ITEMS

In this chapter, we will explore how to add **power-ups** and **special items** to your game, which can enhance the player's abilities and provide exciting rewards. You will learn how to **implement power-ups** like **health boosts, speed boosts**, and **shields, create item pickups** and their effects, **spawn power-ups** in the game world, and handle **item collisions** and basic **inventory systems**. These elements are essential for providing dynamic gameplay and offering players incentives to explore and engage with the game.

Implementing Power-Ups: Health, Speed Boosts, Shields

Power-ups are temporary enhancements that the player can collect during the game. They can help the player by increasing health, boosting speed, or providing shields. Each type of power-up will have its own effect and can be triggered when the player collides with the item.

1. **Health** **Power-up**:

   A health power-up restores the player's health when

picked up. This can be a simple item, such as a health pack or potion.

Example of **health power-up implementation**:

python

```python
class HealthPowerUp(pygame.sprite.Sprite):
    def __init__(self, x, y):
        super().__init__()
        self.image = pygame.Surface((30,
30))
        self.image.fill((255, 0, 0))  # Red
color for health power-up
        self.rect = self.image.get_rect()
        self.rect.x = x
        self.rect.y = y

    def effect(self, player):
        player.health += 10  # Increase the
player's health by 10
        if player.health > 100:  # Limit
health to a maximum of 100
            player.health = 100
```

2. **Speed   Boost   Power-up**:
A speed boost increases the player's movement speed for a short duration, allowing them to move faster.

Example of **speed boost implementation**:

python

```
class
SpeedBoostPowerUp(pygame.sprite.Sprite):
    def __init__(self, x, y):
        super().__init__()
        self.image = pygame.Surface((30,
30))
        self.image.fill((0, 255, 0))    #
Green color for speed boost
        self.rect = self.image.get_rect()
        self.rect.x = x
        self.rect.y = y

    def effect(self, player):
        player.speed += 2    # Increase
player's speed

pygame.time.set_timer(pygame.USEREVENT,
5000)  # Boost lasts for 5 seconds

def reset_speed(player):
    player.speed -= 2   # Reset speed to
normal
```

3. **Shield** **Power-up**:
A shield power-up protects the player from damage for a

short time. This is often used to add a strategic layer to gameplay, as it gives the player a chance to avoid damage.

Example of **shield power-up implementation**:

python

```
class ShieldPowerUp(pygame.sprite.Sprite):
    def __init__(self, x, y):
        super().__init__()
        self.image = pygame.Surface((30,
30))
        self.image.fill((0, 0, 255))    #
Blue color for shield power-up
        self.rect = self.image.get_rect()
        self.rect.x = x
        self.rect.y = y

    def effect(self, player):
        player.is_shielded = True    #
Activate shield

pygame.time.set_timer(pygame.USEREVENT  +
1, 5000)  # Shield lasts for 5 seconds

def deactivate_shield(player):
    player.is_shielded = False    #
Deactivate shield
```

Creating Item Pickups and Item Effects

Once you've created power-up objects like health boosts and shields, the next step is to make them interactable with the player. When the player picks up an item, its effect should be applied to the player, and the item should disappear from the game world.

1. **Creating Item Pickups**: Items can be represented by sprites (images or shapes). When the player's character collides with an item, the item will be **removed** from the screen, and its **effect** will be applied.

   Example of **item pickup**:

   python

   ```python
   class ItemPickup(pygame.sprite.Sprite):
       def __init__(self, x, y, item_type):
           super().__init__()
           self.item_type = item_type
           self.image = pygame.Surface((30,
   30))
           if item_type == "health":
               self.image.fill((255, 0, 0))
   # Red for health
           elif item_type == "speed":
               self.image.fill((0, 255, 0))
   # Green for speed boost
   ```

```python
        elif item_type == "shield":
            self.image.fill((0,  0,  255))
# Blue for shield
        self.rect = self.image.get_rect()
        self.rect.x = x
        self.rect.y = y

    def update(self, player):
        if
self.rect.colliderect(player.rect):   # If
player collides with item
            self.apply_effect(player)
            self.kill()  # Remove item from
the game world

    def apply_effect(self, player):
        if self.item_type == "health":
            health_power_up          =
HealthPowerUp(self.rect.x, self.rect.y)

health_power_up.effect(player)
        elif self.item_type == "speed":
            speed_boost              =
SpeedBoostPowerUp(self.rect.x,
self.rect.y)
            speed_boost.effect(player)
        elif self.item_type == "shield":
            shield                   =
ShieldPowerUp(self.rect.x, self.rect.y)
```

```
shield.effect(player)
```

2. **Item** **Effects**:

When an item is picked up, the corresponding effect is applied to the player. We create separate methods for each effect, such as increasing health, boosting speed, or activating a shield.

Spawning Power-Ups in the Game World

To make the game dynamic, we can **spawn power-ups** at random intervals and locations in the game world. Power-ups should be distributed in areas where the player can find and collect them.

1. **Spawning** **Power-Ups**:

You can spawn power-ups at random positions or trigger them after specific events (e.g., after defeating an enemy or completing a level).

Example of **random power-up spawning**:

python

```python
def spawn_power_up():
    item_type = random.choice(["health",
"speed", "shield"])  # Randomly choose item
type
```

```
    x_pos = random.randint(50, 750)   #
Random x position
    y_pos = random.randint(50, 550)   #
Random y position
    new_item = ItemPickup(x_pos, y_pos,
item_type)
    all_sprites.add(new_item)      # Add
power-up to the sprite group
    item_pickups.add(new_item)     # Add
power-up to a separate group for easy
updates

# Call spawn_power_up() to spawn a new item
randomly
spawn_power_up()
```

2. **Power-Up Spawning Timer**:
You can use a timer to spawn power-ups periodically,
adding variety to the game as the player progresses.

Example of **spawning power-ups periodically**:

python

```
pygame.time.set_timer(pygame.USEREVENT,
5000)  # Trigger every 5 seconds

for event in pygame.event.get():
    if event.type == pygame.USEREVENT:
```

129

```
        spawn_power_up()    # Spawn power-up
every 5 seconds
```

Handling Item Collisions and Inventory Systems

In more advanced games, you might want to implement an **inventory system** where the player can store multiple items, such as health potions, shields, or weapons. For now, we'll focus on handling item **collisions** and applying item effects immediately.

1. **Handling Item Collisions**: We already handled item collisions in the `ItemPickup` class using `colliderect()`. This checks if the player collides with an item and applies the corresponding effect.

2. **Basic Inventory System**: To implement a simple inventory, we can store items in a list or dictionary. The player can **collect** multiple types of power-ups, and each type can be stored in the inventory.

Example of a **simple inventory system**:

```python
python

class Player:
    def __init__(self):
        self.health = 100
        self.speed = 5
        self.shield = False
```

```
        self.inventory  =  {"health":  0,
"speed": 0, "shield": 0}

    def        add_item_to_inventory(self,
item_type):
        self.inventory[item_type] += 1  #
Add the item to the inventory

    def use_item(self, item_type):
        if self.inventory[item_type] > 0:
            if item_type == "health":
                self.health += 10
            elif item_type == "speed":
                self.speed += 2
            elif item_type == "shield":
                self.shield = True
            self.inventory[item_type] -= 1
# Use the item
```

Conclusion

In this chapter, you learned how to **implement power-ups** and **special items** in your game, such as **health boosts, speed boosts,** and **shields.** We covered the process of **creating item pickups, spawning power-ups dynamically** in the game world, and handling **item collisions.** We also introduced a simple **inventory system,** allowing the player to collect and use power-ups.

131

Power-ups are a great way to make your game more engaging by providing the player with rewards and enhancing their abilities. In future chapters, we will continue expanding on this system by adding **advanced power-ups**, **item stacking**, and **inventory management**. Keep experimenting with these ideas to enrich your game and make it more enjoyable for players!

CHAPTER 15

CREATING A MAIN MENU AND PAUSE SCREEN

In this chapter, we will build the **user interface (UI)** for your game, focusing on creating a **main menu** and a **pause screen**. These are essential components for most games, allowing players to start the game, adjust options, pause the game during gameplay, and exit. We'll cover how to design and implement a **main menu**, a **pause screen**, and how to handle user input through **buttons** and **events**. Additionally, we will address the transition between different screens (e.g., from the main menu to the game, and from the game to the pause screen).

Designing a User Interface (UI) for Your Game

The **user interface (UI)** includes all the interactive elements players use to interact with the game, such as **menus**, **buttons**, **sliders**, and **icons**. A good UI should be intuitive, easy to navigate, and aesthetically fitting with the game's theme.

For our game, we'll design a simple **main menu** and **pause menu**. Both menus will have options like **Start Game**, **Options**, and

Quit in the main menu, and **Resume**, **Restart**, and **Quit to Main Menu** in the pause screen.

1. **Main**   **Menu**   **Design**:

   The main menu typically appears when the player first launches the game, offering them the option to start the game, view settings, or quit.

   Example layout for the **Main Menu**:

   o **Start Game**: Starts the game.
   o **Options**: Adjust settings (e.g., sound, controls).
   o **Quit**: Exits the game.

2. **Pause**   **Menu**   **Design**:

   The pause menu appears while the game is running and can be accessed by pressing a **Pause button** (usually **Esc** or **P**). The pause menu typically includes:

   o **Resume**: Resumes gameplay from where it was paused.
   o **Restart**: Restarts the game.
   o **Quit to Main Menu**: Exits the game and returns to the main menu.

Building a Main Menu (Start, Options, Quit)

The main menu will be a simple screen with buttons for starting the game, opening options, and quitting the game. We will use

pygame.Rect to create clickable buttons and check for mouse events to trigger the appropriate actions.

1. **Creating** **Buttons**:

   A button is essentially a **rectangular area** that the user can click on. We will create a function to handle drawing and checking if the mouse click intersects the button.

   Example of creating a **button class**:

   python

```
class Button:
    def __init__(self, x, y, width, height,
text):
        self.rect  =  pygame.Rect(x,  y,
width, height)
        self.color = (0, 128, 255)  #
Button color (blue)
        self.text = text
        self.font = pygame.font.Font(None,
36)  # Font for the button text
        self.text_surface          =
self.font.render(text, True, (255, 255,
255))  # White text
        self.text_rect             =
self.text_surface.get_rect(center=self.re
ct.center)
```

135

```
def draw(self, screen):
    pygame.draw.rect(screen,
self.color, self.rect)  # Draw the button
        screen.blit(self.text_surface,
self.text_rect)  # Draw the button text

    def is_clicked(self, pos):
        return self.rect.collidepoint(pos)
# Check if the mouse click is inside the
button
```

2. **Main Menu Implementation**: Using the `Button` class, we will create buttons for the main menu and handle **click events**.

Example of creating and handling the **main menu**:

python

```
def main_menu():
    start_button = Button(300, 200, 200,
50, "Start Game")
    quit_button = Button(300, 300, 200, 50,
"Quit")
    running = True

    while running:
        for event in pygame.event.get():
            if event.type == pygame.QUIT:
                pygame.quit()
```

```
                        sys.exit()
            elif        event.type        ==
pygame.MOUSEBUTTONDOWN:    # Check if the
player clicks
                if
start_button.is_clicked(event.pos):    # If
the Start button is clicked
                    return    "start"    #
Transition to the game
                elif
quit_button.is_clicked(event.pos):    # If
the Quit button is clicked
                    pygame.quit()
                    sys.exit()


        # Draw the menu screen
        screen.fill((0, 0, 0))    # Black
background
        start_button.draw(screen)   # Draw
the Start button
        quit_button.draw(screen)    # Draw
the Quit button
        pygame.display.update()
```

In this example, when the player clicks **Start Game**, the game will transition to the gameplay screen. If they click **Quit**, the game will close.

137

Creating a Pause Menu and Resuming the Game

Now that we've built a basic main menu, let's create a **pause menu** that the player can access while playing. The pause menu allows the player to **resume** the game, **restart** the game, or **quit** to the main menu.

1. **Pause Menu Implementation**:
   The pause menu will be similar to the main menu but will appear when the game is paused. We will allow the player to press the **Esc key** or click the **Pause button** to toggle the pause state.

   Example of creating and handling the **pause menu**:

   python

   ```python
   def pause_menu():
       resume_button = Button(300, 200, 200,
   50, "Resume")
       restart_button = Button(300, 300, 200,
   50, "Restart")
       quit_button = Button(300, 400, 200, 50,
   "Quit to Main Menu")
       running = True

       while running:
           for event in pygame.event.get():
               if event.type == pygame.QUIT:
   ```

```
                pygame.quit()
                sys.exit()
        elif      event.type      ==
pygame.MOUSEBUTTONDOWN:  # Check for mouse
click
            if
resume_button.is_clicked(event.pos):
                return "resume"     #
Resume the game
            elif
restart_button.is_clicked(event.pos):
                return "restart"    #
Restart the game
            elif
quit_button.is_clicked(event.pos):
                return "quit"  # Quit
to main menu

    # Draw the pause screen
    screen.fill((0, 0, 0))   # Black
background
    resume_button.draw(screen)  # Draw
Resume button
    restart_button.draw(screen)        #
Draw Restart button
    quit_button.draw(screen)   # Draw
Quit button
    pygame.display.update()
```

139

In the game loop, you will use this pause menu when the player presses the **Pause key** (usually **Esc**) or when the game state is toggled.

Handling Buttons, Events, and Transitions Between Screens

1. **Handling   Button   Clicks**:
   The key to handling button clicks is using **mouse events** (pygame.MOUSEBUTTONDOWN) and checking if the mouse pointer intersects the button's **rect**. This is done with the is_clicked() method in the Button class.

2. **Transitioning   Between   Screens**:
   Transitioning between screens (e.g., from the main menu to the game, or from the game to the pause screen) can be achieved by returning values from the menu functions and using those values in the game loop.

   Example of handling **screen transitions**:

   python

   ```python
   game_state = main_menu()   # Get the state
   after the main menu
   if game_state == "start":
       start_game()  # Start the game
   elif game_state == "quit":
       pygame.quit()  # Quit the game
   ```

```
        sys.exit()


# In the game loop:
if is_paused:
    pause_state = pause_menu()
    if pause_state == "resume":
        is_paused = False    # Resume the
game
    elif pause_state == "restart":
        restart_game()   # Restart the game
    elif pause_state == "quit":
        game_state = main_menu()   # Go back
to the main menu
```

By checking the return value of the menu functions (`main_menu()` and `pause_menu()`), you can easily control the flow of the game and switch between screens.

Conclusion

In this chapter, you learned how to build a **main menu** and **pause screen** for your game. You implemented a **Button class** to handle clickable buttons and managed transitions between screens (from the main menu to the game, and from the game to the pause screen). The pause menu allows the player to resume, restart, or quit to the main menu, enhancing the game's user experience.

The ability to design and navigate menus is essential in creating a polished game, and with these skills, you can add more sophisticated UI elements, such as **options menus** or **settings**. In the next chapters, we will continue building on these features, adding **game progression**, **scoreboards**, and more advanced gameplay mechanics.

CHAPTER 16

IMPLEMENTING GAME OVER AND RESTART FEATURES

In this chapter, we will implement essential features that are present in nearly every game: the **game-over screen**, the **restart feature**, and the ability to **save game progress**. These elements help to manage the flow of the game and enhance the player's experience. We will also discuss how to transition smoothly between the **game-over screen** and the **main menu**.

Creating a Game-Over Screen

A **game-over screen** appears when the player's character loses all of their health or when they fail to meet certain game objectives (e.g., reaching the end of the level, defeating a boss). This screen typically gives the player the option to either **restart** the game or **quit** back to the main menu.

1. **Game Over Screen Design**:
   A typical game-over screen might display:
   - A message like "Game Over" or "You Lost!"
   - Options to **Restart** or **Quit to Main Menu**.

o Optionally, display the **final score** or **level reached**.

Example of a **simple game-over screen**:

python

```python
def game_over_screen():
    game_over_text                           =
pygame.font.Font(None,     72).render("Game
Over", True, (255, 0, 0))
    restart_button = Button(300, 200, 200,
50, "Restart")
    quit_button = Button(300, 300, 200, 50,
"Quit to Main Menu")
    running = True

    while running:
        for event in pygame.event.get():
            if event.type == pygame.QUIT:
                pygame.quit()
                sys.exit()
            elif        event.type        ==
pygame.MOUSEBUTTONDOWN:    # Mouse  click
events
                if
restart_button.is_clicked(event.pos):    #
Restart button clicked
                    return "restart"
```

```
                  elif
quit_button.is_clicked(event.pos):   # Quit
button clicked
                 return "quit"


        # Draw game over screen
        screen.fill((0, 0, 0))   # Black
background
        screen.blit(game_over_text,  (250,
100))  # Draw game over text
        restart_button.draw(screen)      #
Draw Restart button
        quit_button.draw(screen)    # Draw
Quit button
        pygame.display.update()
```

In this code:

- The **game over screen** displays a "Game Over" message.
- It includes buttons for **Restart** and **Quit to Main Menu**.
- Based on user input, the game either restarts or transitions back to the main menu.

Implementing a Restart Feature

A **restart feature** allows the player to start the game from the beginning after a **game over**. The restart option should reset the player's health, score, and any other game-specific variables to their initial values.

1. **Restarting the Game**:
   When the player clicks on **Restart**, the game state is reset to the initial conditions, and the game loop starts over.

   Example of **restarting the game**:

   python

   ```python
   def restart_game():
       global player_health, player_score, player_x, player_y
       # Reset game variables
       player_health = 100
       player_score = 0
       player_x, player_y = 100, 500  # Reset player position

       # Reset level or any game state
       reset_level()

       # Transition to gameplay (start a new game)
       start_game()
   ```

2. **Resetting the Level**:
   You can define a **reset_level()** function that resets all

level-related variables, such as enemies, platforms, and other game elements.

Example of **resetting the level**:

python

```
def reset_level():
    global platforms, enemies
    platforms = []   # Reset platforms
    enemies = []   # Reset enemies
    create_level()   # Recreate the level
layout
```

This ensures that every time the player restarts, they play through a fresh version of the level.

Saving Game Progress (Saving Scores, Levels)

Saving game progress is crucial for more complex games where players might want to continue playing at a later time. You can save things like the player's **score**, **level**, and **health**. In simple games, you can save progress using **files** (e.g., JSON or text files) to store important data.

1. **Saving   Scores   and   Levels**:
   We can use Python's `json` module to save and load the

player's progress. You'll save the player's score, level, and health to a file.

Example of **saving progress to a file**:

```python
import json

def save_progress(score, level, health):
    data = {
        'score': score,
        'level': level,
        'health': health
    }

    with open("save_game.json", "w") as file:
        json.dump(data, file)  # Save data to file
```

2. **Loading Saved Progress**: You can load the saved progress when the game starts, allowing the player to continue from where they left off.

Example of **loading saved progress**:

```python
def load_progress():
```

```
try:
    with open("save_game.json", "r")
as file:
        data = json.load(file)  # Load
the saved data
        score = data['score']
        level = data['level']
        health = data['health']
        return score, level, health
except FileNotFoundError:
    return 0, 1, 100  # Default values
if no save file exists
```

When the game starts, you can use `load_progress()` to get the player's saved data and set the game's state accordingly.

Transitioning Between Game Over and Main Menu

After the player has finished a game (either winning or losing), you need to transition smoothly between the **game over screen** and the **main menu**. This involves returning to the main menu after the game ends or when the player chooses to quit.

1. **Handling** **Transitions**:
   In the game loop, when the player reaches **game over**,

you'll call the **game over screen** and check for the player's choice to either restart or quit to the main menu.

Example of **game over handling**:

python

```
def game_loop():
    global game_state
    while True:
        if player_health <= 0:  # Check if
player health is 0
            game_state                    =
game_over_screen()  # Show game over screen
            if game_state == "restart":
                restart_game()  # Restart
the game
            elif game_state == "quit":
                game_state  -  main_menu()
# Go back to main menu
```

This allows the game to **restart** when the player clicks "Restart" or **quit to the main menu** when they click "Quit".

150

Conclusion

In this chapter, we focused on implementing essential **game-over** and **restart** features for your game. You learned how to create a **game-over screen**, implement a **restart feature**, and save and load game progress. These features are important for managing the game flow and ensuring players can restart the game or continue from where they left off.

By adding **game-over screens**, **saving progress**, and **level transitions**, you can create a more polished and interactive experience for your players. In future chapters, we will continue refining the game's mechanics, adding **more levels**, **enemies**, and **advanced features** to enhance gameplay and player engagement.

CHAPTER 17

CREATING A HIGH SCORE SYSTEM

In this chapter, we will implement a **high score system** for your game. High scores are an essential feature in many games, encouraging players to keep playing in order to achieve better results. We'll cover how to **save and display high scores**, **store scores** in a file (or database), **display top scores** after each game session, and **manage scoreboards** and **player rankings**. By the end of this chapter, your game will not only track the player's current score but also save and display the highest scores achieved, providing motivation for players to improve.

Saving and Displaying High Scores

A high score system typically keeps track of the best scores the player has achieved and displays them after each game session. We'll store the high score in a file (e.g., a JSON or text file) so it persists across different sessions of the game. After each game, we will check if the current score is higher than the previous high score and update it if necessary.

1. **Saving the High Score**:
We will use Python's `json` module to save the high score in a file. The file will store the highest score achieved, and we can easily update it after every game session.

Example of **saving high score to a file**:

```python
import json

def save_high_score(score):
    try:
        # Attempt to read the existing high score from the file
        with open("high_score.json", "r") as file:
            data = json.load(file)
            high_score = data['high_score']
    except (FileNotFoundError, json.JSONDecodeError):
        high_score = 0  # If the file doesn't exist or is empty, set the high score to 0

    # Check if the new score is higher than the previous high score
    if score > high_score:
```

153

```
        high_score = score
        with open("high_score.json", "w")
as file:
            json.dump({'high_score':
high_score}, file)    # Save the new high
score
    return high_score
```

In this function:

- o We first attempt to read the existing high score from the `high_score.json` file.
- o If the current score exceeds the stored high score, it will update the file with the new high score.
- o If the file doesn't exist (e.g., the player is playing for the first time), we initialize the high score to 0.

Storing Scores in a File or Database

For most games, storing scores in a **file** is sufficient. However, for more complex systems or if your game involves multiple players or online features, using a **database** may be more appropriate. In this chapter, we will focus on using **files**, but I will explain briefly how this can be extended to a database system.

1. **Storing High Scores in a File**: As shown earlier, storing the high score in a JSON file is simple and effective. It allows you to save and load data easily.

2. **Using a Database for High Scores**: If you need more advanced features, such as **multiple player accounts** or **online scoreboards**, using a database like **SQLite** or **MySQL** would be a better choice. For this chapter, we will continue using file storage for simplicity, but you can extend this with a database when necessary.

   Example of **storing high scores in a file** (already covered in the `save_high_score` function above).

Displaying Top Scores After Each Game Session

Once the high score is saved, you need to display it to the player at the end of the game, so they can see their performance and be motivated to improve.

1. **Displaying the High Score**: After each game session, we will display the player's current score along with the **top score** (the high score). This can be done on the **game-over screen** or the **main menu**.

   Example of **displaying high score**:

```python

def display_high_score(score, screen):
    high_score = save_high_score(score)  # Get the updated high score
    font = pygame.font.Font(None, 36)  # Font for displaying text
    score_text = font.render(f"Your Score: {score}", True, (255, 255, 255))
    high_score_text = font.render(f"High Score: {high_score}", True, (255, 255, 255))

    # Display the score and high score on the screen
    screen.blit(score_text, (300, 200))
    screen.blit(high_score_text, (300, 250))
    pygame.display.update()
```

In this example:

- After the player's game session, the **current score** is displayed alongside the **high score**.
- The `save_high_score()` function is called to ensure that the high score is updated.

Managing Scoreboards and Player Rankings

If you want to expand your game to track the **top players** or display a **scoreboard**, you can store multiple scores (rather than just one high score). This can be done by storing a list of scores and sorting them.

1. **Storing Multiple Scores**: Instead of just keeping a single high score, you can keep a list of the top scores. For example, you could store the **top 5 scores** of all players.

   Example of **storing top scores**:

   python

   ```python
   def save_top_scores(score):
       try:
           with open("scoreboard.json", "r") as file:
               data = json.load(file)
               top_scores = data['top_scores']
       except (FileNotFoundError, json.JSONDecodeError):
           top_scores = []

       # Add the new score and sort the list
   in descending order
   ```

157

```
top_scores.append(score)
top_scores.sort(reverse=True)

# Keep only the top 5 scores
top_scores = top_scores[:5]

with open("scoreboard.json", "w") as
file:
        json.dump({'top_scores':
top_scores}, file)

return top_scores
```

In this code:

- We load the existing **top scores** from the scoreboard.json file.
- We add the current score to the list of scores and sort them in **descending order**.
- We limit the list to the top 5 scores and save it back to the file.

2. **Displaying the Scoreboard**: To display the top scores, you can load the top scores from the file and render them on the screen.

Example of **displaying the scoreboard**:

```python
python
```

```python
def display_scoreboard(screen):
    try:
        with open("scoreboard.json", "r") as file:
            data = json.load(file)
            top_scores = data['top_scores']
    except (FileNotFoundError, json.JSONDecodeError):
        top_scores = []

    font = pygame.font.Font(None, 36)
    screen.fill((0, 0, 0))  # Black background

    # Display the top 5 scores
    for idx, score in enumerate(top_scores):
        score_text = font.render(f"{idx + 1}. {score}", True, (255, 255, 255))
        screen.blit(score_text, (250, 100 + idx * 40))

    pygame.display.update()
```

This code will render the top 5 scores from the **scoreboard** file, displaying each score on the screen.

159

Conclusion

In this chapter, you learned how to implement a **high score system** in your game. We covered how to:

- **Save and display high scores** after each game session.
- **Store scores** in a file (using JSON).
- **Display top scores** and create a **scoreboard** that tracks the highest scores in the game.
- Manage **scoreboard rankings** and display the **top scores** to the player.

By adding these features, you provide players with an incentive to keep playing and improving their performance. In future chapters, you can expand this system to include more advanced features, such as **multiple player profiles**, **online leaderboards**, and **achievements**.

CHAPTER 18

ANIMATION TECHNIQUES FOR SMOOTH MOVEMENT

In this chapter, we will explore how to implement **frame-based animation** for sprites, creating smooth transitions between different **sprite states**, handling **sprite flipping** for animations (like moving left or right), and using **sprite sheets** to optimize memory usage. Animations are essential for making your game feel dynamic and engaging. By the end of this chapter, you'll be able to create smooth, visually appealing animations that improve your game's user experience.

How to Implement Frame-Based Animation for Sprites

In 2D games, **frame-based animation** involves cycling through a series of images (frames) to create the illusion of movement. Each frame represents a slight change from the previous one, and when played in sequence, they appear as continuous motion.

1. **Basic Frame Animation Setup**: A **sprite** can be a character or object in the game that needs to be animated (e.g., walking, jumping). Frame-based animation for a

sprite is done by switching between different frames from a set of images.

Example of **frame-based animation for a sprite**:

python

```python
class Player(pygame.sprite.Sprite):
    def __init__(self):
        super().__init__()
        self.images                              =
[pygame.image.load(f'frame_{i}.png') for i
in  range(1,  5)]    #  Load  4  frames  of
animation
        self.current_frame = 0    # Start
with the first frame
        self.image                               =
self.images[self.current_frame]
        self.rect = self.image.get_rect()
        self.rect.x = 100
        self.rect.y = 300

    def update(self):
        self.current_frame += 1
        if        self.current_frame         >=
len(self.images):  # Loop back to the first
frame
            self.current_frame = 0
```

```
self.image                    =
self.images[self.current_frame]   # Update
the sprite's image
```

In this code:

- o The player sprite has a list of images (`self.images`) representing different frames.
- o `update()` is called each frame to switch between images, creating the animation effect.
- o The **animation loops** back to the first frame once it reaches the end of the image list.

Creating Smooth Transitions Between Different Sprite States

In a game, a sprite might have multiple states (e.g., walking, jumping, idle). When the sprite changes from one state to another, it's important to create smooth transitions between the states. This can be done by switching between different animation frames based on the current state.

1. **Multiple States for the Sprite**: For example, we might want the player to have different animations for walking, jumping, and idle. We can separate the frames for each state into different lists and switch between them depending on the player's actions.

163

Example of smooth transitions between sprite states:

python

```python
class Player(pygame.sprite.Sprite):
    def __init__(self):
        super().__init__()
        # Create separate lists of images
for different states
        self.idle_images          =
[pygame.image.load(f'idle_{i}.png') for i
in range(1, 4)]
        self.walking_images       =
[pygame.image.load(f'walk_{i}.png') for i
in range(1, 6)]
        self.jumping_images       =
[pygame.image.load(f'jump_{i}.png') for i
in range(1, 3)]

        self.state = 'idle'    # Default
state
        self.current_frame = 0
        self.image                =
self.idle_images[self.current_frame]
        self.rect = self.image.get_rect()
        self.rect.x = 100
        self.rect.y = 300

    def update(self):
        if self.state == 'idle':
```

```
        self.current_frame += 1
        if    self.current_frame    >=
len(self.idle_images):
            self.current_frame = 0
        self.image            =
self.idle_images[self.current_frame]
    elif self.state == 'walking':
        self.current_frame += 1
        if    self.current_frame    >=
len(self.walking_images):
            self.current_frame = 0
        self.image            =
self.walking_images[self.current_frame]
    elif self.state == 'jumping':
        self.current_frame += 1
        if    self.current_frame    >=
len(self.jumping_images):
            self.current_frame = 0
        self.image            =
self.jumping_images[self.current_frame]
```

In this code:

- o The player sprite has three states: `idle`,
  `walking`, and `jumping`.
- o Each state has its own list of frames
  (`idle_images`, `walking_images`,
  `jumping_images`).

165

o The **update()** method checks the current state of the player and updates the sprite's animation accordingly.

Handling Sprite Flipping for Animations (Left/Right)

In many games, the player character can move in both directions (left and right). To create a realistic movement effect, we need to **flip the sprite** horizontally when the player moves left or right.

Pygame provides a simple way to **flip** an image using `pygame.transform.flip()`, which takes the image and two arguments: the first for flipping the image horizontally and the second for flipping it vertically.

1. **Flipping the Sprite**: When the player moves to the left, the sprite should face left; when the player moves to the right, the sprite should face right. We can handle this by flipping the sprite's image based on the player's direction.

Example of **flipping the sprite**:

```python
python

class Player(pygame.sprite.Sprite):
    def __init__(self):
        super().__init__()
```

```python
        self.walking_images_right        =
[pygame.image.load(f'walk_right_{i}.png')
for i in range(1, 6)]
        self.walking_images_left         =
[pygame.image.load(f'walk_left_{i}.png')
for i in range(1, 6)]
        self.state = 'idle'
        self.direction = 'right'  # Default
direction is right
        self.current_frame = 0
        self.image                       =
self.walking_images_right[self.current_fr
ame]
        self.rect = self.image.get_rect()
        self.rect.x = 100
        self.rect.y = 300

    def update(self):
        if self.state == 'walking':
            self.current_frame += 1
            if    self.current_frame    >=
len(self.walking_images_right):
                self.current_frame = 0

            if self.direction == 'right':
                self.image               =
self.walking_images_right[self.current_fr
ame]
            else:  # If moving left
```

167

```
        self.image              =
self.walking_images_left[self.current_fra
me]


        if  self.rect.x  <  0:      #  Flip
direction  when  player  reaches  the  left
boundary
            self.direction = 'right'
            self.rect.x = 0
        elif self.rect.x > 800:    #  Flip
direction  when  player  reaches  the  right
boundary
            self.direction = 'left'
            self.rect.x = 800
```

In this example:

- o The `walking_images_right` and `walking_images_left` lists contain the frames for walking in both directions.

- o The **update()** method checks the `direction` of the player and flips the sprite accordingly.

- o The player will move in the direction they are facing, and the sprite will be flipped automatically when moving in the opposite direction.

Using Sprite Sheets to Optimize Memory Usage

When creating a game with many animations, storing individual images for each frame can quickly become inefficient in terms of memory usage. A **sprite sheet** is a single image file that contains multiple frames of animation arranged in a grid. Using a sprite sheet can reduce the number of files you need to load and optimize memory usage.

1. **Loading Frames from a Sprite Sheet**: To use a sprite sheet, we need to extract individual frames from the large image and display them in sequence. We can do this by using the subsurface() method, which allows us to define a rectangular region of the sprite sheet.

   Example of **loading frames from a sprite sheet**:

   python

```python
class Player(pygame.sprite.Sprite):
    def __init__(self):
        super().__init__()
        sprite_sheet                =
pygame.image.load("player_spritesheet.png
")
        self.frame_width = 50
        self.frame_height = 50
        self.frames = []
```

169

```python
        # Extract frames from the sprite
sheet
        for i in range(4):   # Assuming
there are 4 frames in a row
            frame                    =
sprite_sheet.subsurface(pygame.Rect(i    *
self.frame_width,   0,   self.frame_width,
self.frame_height))
            self.frames.append(frame)

        self.current_frame = 0
        self.image                   =
self.frames[self.current_frame]
        self.rect = self.image.get_rect()
        self.rect.x = 100
        self.rect.y = 300

    def update(self):
        self.current_frame += 1
        if       self.current_frame       >=
len(self.frames):
            self.current_frame = 0
        self.image                   =
self.frames[self.current_frame]
```

In this code:

- o We load a **sprite** **sheet** (`player_spritesheet.png`) and use `subsurface()` to extract each frame.
- o Each frame is stored in a list (`self.frames`), and the **update()** method cycles through these frames to create the animation effect.

2. **Using Sprite Sheets Efficiently**:
   - o Store multiple animations (e.g., walking, jumping) in one sprite sheet.
   - o Load and cut out frames from the sprite sheet dynamically as needed.

Conclusion

In this chapter, we learned how to implement **frame-based animation** for sprites, handle **sprite flipping** for movement directions (left and right), and use **sprite sheets** to optimize memory usage. By using these animation techniques, you can create smooth, dynamic animations that bring your game to life.

As your game grows, you can expand on these concepts by adding more complex animations for various actions (e.g., **attacking, dying, interacting with objects**) and using advanced sprite sheet techniques to efficiently manage resources. In the next chapters, we will continue refining the game's mechanics and adding more engaging features!

CHAPTER 19

BUILDING YOUR FIRST PUZZLE GAME

In this chapter, we will build a **simple puzzle game**. Puzzle games are popular for their ability to engage the player with challenges that test their logic, memory, and problem-solving skills. We will create a puzzle game that can be a **sliding puzzle** (like a 3x3 grid with one empty slot, where the player moves tiles to complete the picture) or a **memory match** game (where the player matches pairs of cards). We will cover how to design the puzzle, implement the logic for puzzle pieces, handle user input, and add win/lose conditions.

By the end of this chapter, you'll have a basic, interactive puzzle game where the player can attempt to solve puzzles, and the game will display a win or lose message depending on the outcome.

Designing a Simple Puzzle Game

First, let's choose the type of puzzle game we'll create. For this chapter, we'll focus on two possible types of puzzles:

1. **Sliding**   **Puzzle**:

   A sliding puzzle typically involves a grid of tiles (e.g., 3x3), where the player can move tiles to rearrange them in the correct order. One slot will be empty, allowing the player to slide adjacent tiles into that space.

2. **Memory**   **Match**   **Game**:

   A memory match game consists of pairs of cards faced down. The player flips over two cards at a time and tries to match them. If the cards match, they remain face up; if not, they are flipped back.

For simplicity, we will start by creating a **sliding puzzle** game, which will give us a great foundation to handle the puzzle pieces and manage user input.

Implementing Logic for Puzzle Pieces

To start, we will need to represent the puzzle as a grid of tiles. We can do this using **pygame.Rect** objects, where each tile will be a rectangle. The key to the sliding puzzle is that one tile will be **empty** at all times, allowing the player to move adjacent tiles into the empty space.

1. **Representing Puzzle Pieces**: Each tile is an individual part of the puzzle, and they are arranged in a grid. When

a player clicks on a tile adjacent to the empty space, that tile will move into the empty slot.

Example of **representing puzzle tiles**:

python

```python
class PuzzlePiece(pygame.sprite.Sprite):
    def __init__(self, x, y, width, height,
image, correct_position):
        super().__init__()
        self.image = image  # Image for the
puzzle piece (tile)
        self.rect = self.image.get_rect()
        self.rect.x = x
        self.rect.y = y
        self.correct_position          =
correct_position   #  The  correct  (x,  y)
position of the tile
        self.position = (x, y)   # Current
position of the tile

    def move(self, new_x, new_y):
        self.rect.x = new_x
        self.rect.y = new_y
        self.position = (new_x, new_y)

    def is_correct(self):
```

```
        return       self.position       ==
self.correct_position  # Check if the piece
is in the correct spot
```

In this class:

- o   x, y represent the current position of the puzzle piece.
- o   correct_position is where the piece should be after the puzzle is solved.
- o   move() is used to move a piece into a new position, and is_correct() checks if the piece is in its correct location.

2. **Grid   Setup**:

We'll create the grid of tiles and the empty space, using a 3x3 grid (9 tiles in total). The tiles will have images, and one slot will be left empty to allow for movement.

Example of **grid setup**:

```
python

def create_puzzle():
    puzzle_pieces = pygame.sprite.Group()
    piece_images                          =
[pygame.image.load(f"tile_{i}.png")  for  i
in range(9)]  # Load 9 images for the tiles
```

```
    correct_positions = [(x, y) for x in
range(3) for y in range(3)]  # Correct
positions in a 3x3 grid

    for i in range(8):  # Only 8 pieces,
leaving the last one empty
        x = (i % 3) * 100  # Tile x position
        y = (i // 3) * 100   # Tile y
position
        puzzle_piece = PuzzlePiece(x, y,
100,        100,       piece_images[i],
correct_positions[i])
        puzzle_pieces.add(puzzle_piece)

    # Create an empty slot at the last
position
    empty_slot = PuzzlePiece(200, 200,
100, 100, None, (2, 2))  # Empty slot at
(2,2)
    puzzle_pieces.add(empty_slot)

    return puzzle_pieces
```

In this function:

- o   We load 9 images (tile_0.png, tile_1.png, etc.) for the puzzle pieces.
- o   We set the correct positions of each tile in the grid.

177

    o   The empty slot is added at position (2, 2) in the grid.

Handling User Input for Puzzle Completion

To interact with the puzzle, we need to handle **user input**. When the player clicks on a tile adjacent to the empty space, the game should move that tile into the empty slot. We will also check whether the puzzle has been solved after each move.

1. **Handling Tile Movement**: The player can click on a tile, and if it is adjacent to the empty slot, it will move into the empty space.

   Example of **handling tile movement**:

   python

```python
def handle_click(puzzle_pieces,
mouse_pos):
    for piece in puzzle_pieces:
        if
piece.rect.collidepoint(mouse_pos):
            empty_slot           =
find_empty_slot(puzzle_pieces)
            if         is_adjacent(piece,
empty_slot):  # Check if the clicked piece
is adjacent to the empty slot
```

```
            move_piece(piece,
empty_slot)  # Move the piece to the empty
slot

check_if_solved(puzzle_pieces)

def find_empty_slot(puzzle_pieces):
    for piece in puzzle_pieces:
        if piece.image is None:   # The
empty slot has no image
            return piece

def is_adjacent(piece, empty_slot):
    piece_x, piece_y = piece.position
    empty_x, empty_y = empty_slot.position
    return (abs(piece_x - empty_x) == 100
and piece_y == empty_y) or (abs(piece_y -
empty_y) == 100 and piece_x == empty_x)

def move_piece(piece, empty_slot):
    empty_slot.move(piece.rect.x,
piece.rect.y)
    piece.move(empty_slot.rect.x,
empty_slot.rect.y)
```

In this code:

- **handle_click()** checks if the player clicked on a tile.

- **is_adjacent()** checks if the clicked piece is adjacent to the empty slot.
- **move_piece()** swaps the positions of the clicked tile and the empty slot.
- **check_if_solved()** checks whether the puzzle has been completed.

2. **Checking for Puzzle Completion**: After each move, we need to check if all the pieces are in their correct positions.

   Example of **checking if the puzzle is solved**:

   python

```python
def check_if_solved(puzzle_pieces):
    for piece in puzzle_pieces:
        if not piece.is_correct():   # If
any piece is not in the correct position
            return False
    display_win_message()  # If all pieces
are in the correct position
    return True
```

Adding a Win/Lose Condition

The win condition for a sliding puzzle is simple: the puzzle is solved when all the pieces are in their correct positions. If the player manages to arrange all the tiles correctly, the game will display a **win message**.

1. **Displaying a Win Message**: When the puzzle is solved, we can display a message like "You Win!" and offer the player the option to **restart** the puzzle or **return to the main menu**.

   Example of **win message**:

   python

   ```python
   def display_win_message():
       font = pygame.font.Font(None, 72)
       win_text = font.render("You Win!",
   True, (0, 255, 0))
       screen.blit(win_text, (300, 200))  #
   Display the win message at (300, 200)
       pygame.display.update()
   ```

2. **Restarting the Puzzle**: After winning, the player can restart the puzzle or return to the main menu. This can be done with a simple prompt and event handling.

Conclusion

In this chapter, you learned how to create a **simple puzzle game**. We implemented the logic for puzzle pieces, handling **user input** to move tiles, and checking for **puzzle completion**. We also added a **win/lose condition** to allow the player to finish the puzzle and restart the game if desired.

With these building blocks, you can expand your puzzle game by adding different types of puzzles (e.g., **memory match**, **jigsaw puzzles**, or **maze puzzles**) and increasing the complexity with more advanced features such as **timer-based challenges** or **multiplayer functionality**.

Puzzle games are a great way to engage players with logical challenges and problem-solving tasks. By refining and expanding upon these mechanics, you can create more complex and interesting puzzle games for players to enjoy!

CHAPTER 20

CREATING A 2D SHOOTER GAME

In this chapter, we will build a **2D shooter game** where the player can **shoot bullets**, **aim** at enemies, and **destroy enemies** when hit. We will also add **shooting power-ups** and **weapon upgrades** to make the gameplay more exciting and dynamic. Finally, we will implement **collision detection** between bullets and enemies to determine when a bullet hits an enemy and causes damage or destruction.

By the end of this chapter, you'll have a fully functional 2D shooter game where the player can shoot at enemies, collect power-ups, and upgrade weapons for more powerful attacks.

Setting Up Shooting Mechanics (Bullets, Aiming)

To create the shooting mechanics, we will need to allow the player to shoot bullets, aim at enemies, and have the bullets move in the direction the player is facing.

1. **Creating** **Bullet** **Class**:
   A bullet is a simple **sprite** that moves across the screen when the player shoots it. The bullet should be created at

the player's position and move in the direction they are aiming.

Example of a **Bullet class**:

python

```python
class Bullet(pygame.sprite.Sprite):
    def __init__(self, x, y, direction):
        super().__init__()
        self.image = pygame.Surface((10, 5))  # Bullet size
        self.image.fill((255, 0, 0))  # Red color for the bullet
        self.rect = self.image.get_rect()
        self.rect.x = x
        self.rect.y = y
        self.direction = direction  # Direction the bullet moves in (left, right, up, down)
        self.speed = 10

    def update(self):
        if self.direction == "right":
            self.rect.x += self.speed  # Move the bullet to the right
        elif self.direction == "left":
            self.rect.x -= self.speed  # Move the bullet to the left
```

```
        elif self.direction == "up":
            self.rect.y -= self.speed    #
Move the bullet up
        elif self.direction == "down":
            self.rect.y += self.speed    #
Move the bullet down
```

In this class:

- o The bullet's **direction** is passed when it is created, allowing it to move in any of the four directions: **left, right, up,** or **down.**
- o The **update()** method moves the bullet in the appropriate direction based on the direction it was assigned.

2. **Aiming** **and** **Shooting**: The player will shoot by pressing a key (e.g., **spacebar**), and the bullet will move in the direction the player is facing. The player can move around the screen and shoot in multiple directions.

Example of **shooting and aiming**:

```
python

player_direction = "right"  # The direction
the player is facing
```

```
if keys[pygame.K_LEFT]:   # If the left
arrow key is pressed
    player_direction = "left"
elif keys[pygame.K_RIGHT]:  # If the right
arrow key is pressed
    player_direction = "right"
elif keys[pygame.K_UP]:  # If the up arrow
key is pressed
    player_direction = "up"
elif keys[pygame.K_DOWN]:   # If the down
arrow key is pressed
    player_direction = "down"

if keys[pygame.K_SPACE]:  # Shoot with the
spacebar
    bullet = Bullet(player_x, player_y,
player_direction)
    all_sprites.add(bullet)   # Add the
bullet to the sprite group
```

This code checks the direction the player is facing and shoots a bullet in that direction when the **spacebar** is pressed.

Creating Enemies That Can Be Destroyed

Enemies in a shooter game are typically moving objects that the player must shoot and destroy. These enemies will also be

186

represented as sprites and will move in various directions. When a bullet hits an enemy, the enemy will be destroyed.

1. **Enemy   Class**:

    The enemy will be a sprite that moves across the screen and checks for collisions with bullets. If a collision occurs, the enemy will be destroyed.

    Example of an **Enemy class**:

    python

```python
class Enemy(pygame.sprite.Sprite):
    def __init__(self, x, y):
        super().__init__()
        self.image = pygame.Surface((50,
50))  # Enemy size
        self.image.fill((0, 255, 0))    #
Green color for the enemy
        self.rect = self.image.get_rect()
        self.rect.x = x
        self.rect.y = y
        self.speed = 3

    def update(self):
        self.rect.x -= self.speed   # Move
the enemy to the left
        if self.rect.x < 0:  # If the enemy
moves off-screen
```

```
        self.rect.x = 800  # Reset the
enemy's position to the right side of the
screen

    def destroy(self):
        self.kill()  # Remove the enemy
from the sprite group
```

In this class:

- o The **update()** method moves the enemy from right to left across the screen.
- o The **destroy()** method removes the enemy from the game when it is hit by a bullet.

2. **Collision**   **Detection**:
We need to check for **collisions** between bullets and enemies. If a bullet collides with an enemy, the bullet and the enemy should be destroyed.

Example of **bullet-enemy collision**:

python

```
for bullet in bullets:
    for enemy in enemies:
        if
bullet.rect.colliderect(enemy.rect):  # If
the bullet collides with the enemy
```

```
        bullet.kill()   # Destroy the
bullet
        enemy.destroy()  # Destroy the
enemy
        score += 10   # Increase the
score
```

This code checks each bullet for collisions with each enemy. If a collision is detected, the bullet and enemy are destroyed, and the score is increased.

Implementing Shooting Power-Ups and Weapon Upgrades

To make the shooting mechanics more engaging, we can add **power-ups** and **weapon upgrades**. These can modify the player's shooting abilities, such as increasing the firing rate, changing bullet types, or adding additional bullets.

1. **Creating a Power-Up Class**: A power-up can be a sprite that the player can collect to enhance their weapons. For example, a **fire rate power-up** increases the number of bullets shot per second, and a **spread shot power-up** fires multiple bullets at once.

   Example of a **power-up class**:

   python

```python
class PowerUp(pygame.sprite.Sprite):
    def __init__(self, x, y, power_type):
        super().__init__()
        self.image = pygame.Surface((30,
30))  # Power-up size
        self.image.fill((255, 255, 0))  #
Yellow color for power-ups
        self.rect = self.image.get_rect()
        self.rect.x = x
        self.rect.y = y
        self.power_type = power_type  #
Type of power-up (e.g., "fire_rate",
"spread_shot")

    def apply(self, player):
        if self.power_type == "fire_rate":
            player.fire_rate += 0.2  #
Increase firing rate
        elif self.power_type ==
"spread_shot":
            player.spread_shot = True  #
Enable spread shot
        self.kill()  # Destroy the power-
up after it is applied
```

2. **Handling Power-Up Collision**: When the player collides with a power-up, the corresponding power-up effect will be applied to the player's weapon.

190

Example of **applying a power-up**:

```python
for power_up in power_ups:
    if
player.rect.colliderect(power_up.rect):   #
If the player collects the power-up
        power_up.apply(player)     # Apply
the power-up to the player's weapon
```

Handling Collisions Between Bullets and Enemies

Finally, we need to check for collisions between the player's **bullets** and the **enemies**. When a bullet hits an enemy, both the bullet and the enemy should be destroyed, and the player should receive points for the kill.

1. **Bullet-Enemy   Collision   Handling**:
   This process was covered earlier, where we check each bullet's position and see if it intersects with any enemy. If a collision occurs, the bullet and enemy are destroyed, and the score is increased.

Conclusion

In this chapter, we learned how to create a **2D shooter game**. You've implemented:

- **Shooting mechanics**, allowing the player to shoot bullets and aim at enemies.
- **Enemies that can be destroyed** when hit by bullets.
- **Shooting power-ups and weapon upgrades** to make the gameplay more dynamic and exciting.
- **Collision detection** between bullets and enemies to handle the destruction of enemies and bullets.

With these foundational mechanics in place, you can expand your 2D shooter by adding more **weapon upgrades**, **enemy types**, and **power-ups**. You can also improve the game by adding **sound effects**, **background music**, and more **advanced AI** for enemies. In future chapters, we will continue building on this game by introducing **levels**, **boss fights**, and **scoring systems** to create a more complete and engaging experience.

CHAPTER 21

OPTIMIZING YOUR GAME: TIPS AND TRICKS

As you continue to build your game, you'll encounter performance challenges, especially as the game grows in complexity with more assets, sprites, and game logic. In this chapter, we'll explore how to **optimize game performance**, focusing on improving **frame rate**, managing **memory usage**, handling **large sprite sheets**, reducing **lag and stutter**, and optimizing **event handling**. By implementing these techniques, you can ensure that your game runs smoothly on a variety of devices and provides a seamless experience for players.

Improving Game Performance (Frame Rate, Memory Usage)

1. **Frame Rate Optimization**: The **frame rate** (FPS) is a critical factor in how smooth your game feels. If the frame rate is too low, the game will feel choppy, while a high frame rate will ensure fluid animations and responsiveness. To improve performance, it's important to limit the frame rate to a target number, such as 60 FPS, and optimize the game's logic to run efficiently.

Pygame provides a way to control the frame rate using `pygame.time.Clock()`. This allows you to cap the frame rate and avoid unnecessary performance hits caused by high FPS values.

Example of **capping the frame rate**:

```python
clock = pygame.time.Clock()

while running:
    clock.tick(60)  # Cap the frame rate to
60 FPS
    # Game logic and rendering here
```

This ensures the game runs at a consistent 60 FPS, preventing unnecessary strain on the system's CPU and GPU.

2. **Memory Usage Optimization**: Large game assets, like high-resolution images or audio files, can consume a lot of memory, potentially slowing down the game. To reduce memory usage, you should:

   o **Resize images** to the smallest size needed for display.

- o Use **compressed image formats** (like PNG for sprites with transparency or JPEG for backgrounds) to reduce file size.
- o **Unload unused assets** from memory when they are no longer needed (e.g., when a level is completed or a scene changes).

Example of **image resizing**:

python

```
image                            =
pygame.image.load("large_image.png")
image   =   pygame.transform.scale(image,
(width, height))  # Resize image to fit the
screen or required size
```

Audio: For background music and sound effects, use compressed formats like **MP3** or **OGG** to save memory. Also, consider **streaming** audio files instead of loading them entirely into memory if they are large.

Handling Large Sprite Sheets and Multiple Assets

1. **Using Large Sprite Sheets Efficiently**: A sprite sheet is a single image containing multiple frames of animation. Although sprite sheets can significantly reduce the

number of individual image files, they can become large, leading to high memory usage. To optimize this, you can **load only the frames you need** for a particular animation or action instead of loading the entire sprite sheet.

o **Load only visible frames**: If your game uses animations that don't require all frames at once, load only the frames that are currently being used.

Example of **loading specific frames from a sprite sheet**:

```python
sprite_sheet                               =
pygame.image.load("spritesheet.png")
frame_width = 64
frame_height = 64

def get_frame(row, col):
    return
sprite_sheet.subsurface(pygame.Rect(col    *
frame_width,      row     *      frame_height,
frame_width, frame_height))

# Example: Load specific frames
walking_frame_1 = get_frame(0, 0)  # First
frame in the sprite sheet
walking_frame_2 = get_frame(0, 1)  # Second
frame in the sprite sheet
```

2. **Using Image Atlases**: Instead of using separate image files for each asset, you can create an **image atlas**, which is a large image that contains multiple smaller images (like icons, buttons, etc.). This reduces the number of files your game needs to load and improves rendering efficiency.

Example of using an image atlas:

python

```
atlas = pygame.image.load("atlas.png")
icon = atlas.subsurface(pygame.Rect(0, 0,
32, 32))  # Extract a 32x32 section for the
icon
```

Reducing Lag and Stutter During Gameplay

Lag and stutter in gameplay can occur due to high CPU or GPU usage, especially when there are many moving sprites, complex physics calculations, or large asset files. To reduce lag and stutter, you can:

1. **Optimize Game Logic**: Avoid performing heavy calculations every frame. For example, use **delta time** to smooth out animations and movements, which ensures consistent behavior across different frame rates.

Example of **using delta time** for smooth movement:

```python
last_time = pygame.time.get_ticks()

while running:
    current_time = pygame.time.get_ticks()
    delta_time    =    (current_time    -
last_time) / 1000  # Time passed in seconds
    last_time = current_time

    # Use delta_time to adjust movement
speed
    player_x += player_speed * delta_time
```

2. **Reduce the Number of Sprites**: If you have a lot of sprites on the screen (e.g., in large levels or battles), consider **limiting the number of active sprites** at any given time. You can hide off-screen sprites or **use a culling system** that only renders visible objects.

Example of **sprite culling**:

```python
for sprite in all_sprites:
    if
sprite.rect.colliderect(camera_rect):    #
```

```
Only update and draw sprites within the
camera view
        sprite.update()
        sprite.draw(screen)
```

Optimizing Event Handling and Updates for Better Performance

Event handling and updating every game object each frame can be a significant performance bottleneck. Optimizing these operations is key to maintaining high performance.

1. **Efficient Event Handling**: In Pygame, event handling (`pygame.event.get()`) can become slow if the game constantly checks for unnecessary events. You can reduce the overhead by filtering events early and only handling those that matter.

   Example of **optimizing event handling**:

   python

   ```python
   for event in pygame.event.get():
       if event.type == pygame.QUIT:
           running = False
       elif event.type == pygame.KEYDOWN and
   event.key == pygame.K_SPACE:
           # Handle spacebar press
           handle_spacebar()
   ```

2. **Optimizing Updates**: When updating objects in the game (like moving enemies or checking for collisions), try to reduce the frequency of updates for objects that are not currently active or important. For instance, if an enemy is far from the player and doesn't need to move, you can skip updating its position until it's closer.

Example of **optimized object updates**:

```python
for enemy in enemies:
    if
player.rect.colliderect(enemy.rect):    #
Only  update  enemies  that  are  near  the
player
        enemy.update()
```

Conclusion

In this chapter, we discussed **optimizing your game** for better performance by focusing on key aspects such as **frame rate**, **memory usage**, handling **large sprite sheets**, and reducing **lag and stutter**. We also explored how to optimize **event handling** and **object updates** for smoother gameplay.

Implementing these optimizations will help ensure that your game runs efficiently on a wide range of devices, providing a smooth and enjoyable experience for players. Remember, performance optimization is an ongoing process. As your game grows in complexity, continue to profile and optimize your code to keep it running efficiently. In the next chapters, we'll focus on more advanced techniques to improve gameplay, add more complex features, and continue refining your game.

CHAPTER 22

POLISHING YOUR GAME: GRAPHICS AND UI ENHANCEMENTS

In this chapter, we will focus on enhancing the **visual appeal** and **user experience (UX)** of your game. We'll discuss how to add **visual effects** like explosions and particle effects, **improve game menus** and **UI components**, and **enhance the game's look and feel** using shadows, lighting, and color schemes. Finally, we will explore ways to design a **smooth user experience** that ensures players enjoy interacting with your game.

By the end of this chapter, your game will not only function well but also have a polished and professional appearance that keeps players engaged and immersed in the gameplay.

Adding Visual Effects (Explosions, Particle Effects)

Visual effects like **explosions**, **particle effects**, and other animations can make your game feel more dynamic and exciting. These effects add **flair** to gameplay events like defeating enemies, collecting items, or triggering power-ups. In Pygame, you can create these effects using sprite animations and particle systems.

1. **Explosions**: An explosion can be simulated by displaying a series of **explosion images** that expand and fade out. You can animate the explosion by cycling through a set of frames.

   Example of **explosion effect**:

   python

```python
class Explosion(pygame.sprite.Sprite):
    def __init__(self, x, y):
        super().__init__()
        self.images                      =
[pygame.image.load(f"explosion_{i}.png")
for i in range(1, 6)]  # Explosion frames
        self.current_frame = 0
        self.image                       =
self.images[self.current_frame]
        self.rect = self.image.get_rect()
        self.rect.center = (x, y)
        self.lifetime = 10  # How long the
explosion lasts

    def update(self):
        self.lifetime -= 1
```

```
            if self.lifetime <= 0:   # Destroy
the explosion after it finishes
                self.kill()
        else:
            self.current_frame += 1
            if    self.current_frame    >=
len(self.images):
                self.current_frame    =
len(self.images) - 1  # Keep the last frame
            self.image              =
self.images[self.current_frame]
```

In this code:

- o   The **Explosion** class loads multiple images for each frame of the explosion.
- o   The **update()** method changes the frame of the explosion every time it's called, creating the animation effect.

2. **Particle Effects**: Particle effects are small, moving objects that simulate phenomena like fire, smoke, or magic spells. These are usually random and disappear after a short duration. You can create particles by making small **circle-shaped sprites** that move and fade away.

Example of **particle effect**:

python

```
class Particle(pygame.sprite.Sprite):
    def __init__(self, x, y):
        super().__init__()
        self.image = pygame.Surface((5,
5))  # Small particle size
        self.image.fill((255, 255, 0))  #
Yellow color
        self.rect = self.image.get_rect()
        self.rect.center = (x, y)
        self.velocity                =
pygame.math.Vector2(random.uniform(-1, 1),
random.uniform(-1, 1)) * 2  # Random
direction

    def update(self):
        self.rect.x += self.velocity.x
        self.rect.y += self.velocity.y
        self.image.set_alpha(max(0,
self.image.get_alpha() - 5))  # Fade the
particle
        if self.image.get_alpha() == 0:
            self.kill()  # Remove the
particle once it fades out
```

This example creates a **Particle** class that generates small, moving particles with random directions. The particles fade over time, giving the effect of smoke or debris.

Improving Game Menus and UI Components

A game's **UI** (user interface) plays a huge role in making the experience intuitive and enjoyable. To improve the UI, we can focus on elements like buttons, menus, score displays, and status bars.

1. **Creating Buttons**: Buttons are one of the most common UI components. They should be responsive to user clicks and provide feedback (e.g., change color when hovered over).

   Example of **improving button interaction**:

   python

```python
class Button(pygame.sprite.Sprite):
    def __init__(self, x, y, width, height,
text):
        super().__init__()
        self.rect = pygame.Rect(x, y,
width, height)
        self.text = text
        self.font = pygame.font.Font(None,
36)
        self.text_surface =
self.font.render(text, True, (255, 255,
255))
```

```
        self.text_rect                    =
self.text_surface.get_rect(center=self.re
ct.center)
        self.color_normal = (0, 128, 255)
        self.color_hover = (0, 180, 255)
        self.color = self.color_normal

    def draw(self, screen):
        pygame.draw.rect(screen,
self.color, self.rect)   # Draw the button
        screen.blit(self.text_surface,
self.text_rect)   # Draw the text

    def is_clicked(self, pos):
        return self.rect.collidepoint(pos)

    def update(self, pos):
        if self.rect.collidepoint(pos):   #
Hover effect
            self.color = self.color_hover
        else:
            self.color = self.color_normal
```

In this code:

- o The Button class changes its color when hovered over, providing visual feedback.
- o update() checks the mouse position to apply the hover effect.

2. **Displaying Scores and Game Status**: Game menus should also display important information, like the current score or level. You can use **pygame.font** to render text, and update it dynamically as the game progresses.

Example of **displaying score**:

```python
python
```

```python
def display_score(score):
    font = pygame.font.Font(None, 36)
    score_text = font.render(f"Score:
{score}", True, (255, 255, 255))
    screen.blit(score_text, (10, 10))   #
Display score in the top-left corner
```

Enhancing the Game's Look and Feel with Shadows, Lighting, and Color Schemes

To make your game feel more polished, you can enhance the **visual design** by adding **shadows**, **lighting effects**, and choosing a cohesive **color scheme**.

1. **Shadows**: Adding shadows behind objects can make them feel like they are part of the scene rather than floating in space. Shadows add depth and realism to 2D games.

Example of **adding shadows**:

python

```
def    draw_with_shadow(image,    position,
shadow_offset=(5, 5)):
    shadow_color = (0, 0, 0)  # Black color
for the shadow
    shadow_rect                        =
image.get_rect(topleft=(position[0]     +
shadow_offset[0],       position[1]     +
shadow_offset[1]))
    screen.blit(image,   shadow_rect)     #
Draw the shadow
    screen.blit(image, position)    # Draw
the main image
```

This function **draws a shadow** behind the object by offsetting its position and drawing it in black, followed by the actual image.

2. **Lighting Effects**: Adding lighting effects can create a mood and enhance gameplay. A simple way to simulate lighting is to overlay a **gradient** or **faded circle** that represents a light source.

Example of **simple lighting effect**:

python

```
def draw_lighting(x, y, radius):
    surface                    =
pygame.Surface((screen_width,
screen_height), pygame.SRCALPHA)
    pygame.draw.circle(surface, (255, 255,
255, 50), (x, y), radius)  # Light effect
with transparency
    screen.blit(surface,      (0,      0),
special_flags=pygame.BLEND_RGBA_ADD)
```

This method uses **transparency** to overlay a soft light effect on the screen.

3. **Color Schemes**: Choose a color scheme that fits the theme of your game. Consistent use of colors helps with **branding** and **visual appeal**. For example, a **dark theme** with contrasting bright colors can work well for action games, while a **pastel theme** is better for casual or puzzle games.

    Example of **creating a color scheme**:

    python

```
PRIMARY_COLOR = (0, 128, 255)
SECONDARY_COLOR = (255, 255, 255)
BACKGROUND_COLOR = (20, 20, 20)   # Dark
background for a more intense atmosphere
```

Designing a Smooth User Experience (UX)

A **smooth user experience (UX)** is about making the game intuitive, enjoyable, and accessible. Key UX considerations include **easy navigation**, **responsive controls**, and **clear feedback** on player actions.

1. **Simple and Clear Menus**: Menus should be easy to navigate, with clearly labeled buttons and options. The player should never feel lost or frustrated with navigating the game.

   Example of **simple menu layout**:

   python

```python
def main_menu():
    start_button = Button(300, 200, 200,
50, "Start Game")
    quit_button = Button(300, 300, 200, 50,
"Quit")
    running = True
    while running:
        for event in pygame.event.get():
            if event.type == pygame.QUIT:
                pygame.quit()
                sys.exit()
```

```
            elif        event.type        ==
pygame.MOUSEBUTTONDOWN:
                if
start_button.is_clicked(event.pos):
                    return "start"
            elif
quit_button.is_clicked(event.pos):
                pygame.quit()
                sys.exit()


start_button.update(pygame.mouse.get_pos(
))


quit_button.update(pygame.mouse.get_pos()
)


        screen.fill((0,   0,   0))        #
Background
        start_button.draw(screen)
        quit_button.draw(screen)
        pygame.display.update()
```

This ensures the buttons are **responsive** and **easy to click**, providing feedback when the player hovers over them.

2. **Clear Visual Feedback**: Feedback should be given for player actions. For example, when the player clicks a button, it should change color or give an indication that the click was registered.

212

Example of **visual feedback** on button hover:

```python
python

start_button.update(pygame.mouse.get_pos(
))    # Change color on hover
```

Conclusion

In this chapter, we explored how to polish your game by adding **visual effects**, enhancing **game menus** and **UI components**, and improving the overall **look and feel** with shadows, lighting, and color schemes. We also discussed the importance of designing a **smooth user experience (UX)** by creating intuitive menus, responsive controls, and clear visual feedback.

By implementing these techniques, your game will not only perform well but also offer a **visually appealing** and **user-friendly experience**. As you continue refining your game, remember that polishing your graphics and UI is an ongoing process that will greatly enhance the overall player experience.

CHAPTER 23

DEBUGGING AND TESTING YOUR GAME

In this chapter, we will explore how to **debug** and **test** your game effectively to ensure that it runs smoothly and that all features work as expected. Debugging is essential for identifying and fixing **bugs** (errors in the code), while testing ensures that the game's functionality is consistent and stable. We will cover several techniques for **debugging Python code**, common errors in game development, how to **write unit tests**, and how to **run your game through different test scenarios**.

By the end of this chapter, you'll be able to debug and test your game systematically, ensuring a smooth and error-free player experience.

Techniques for Debugging Python Code

Debugging is the process of identifying and fixing issues in your code. In game development, bugs can occur in various parts of the game, from user input handling to animation logic. Here are some common debugging techniques in Python:

1. **Using `print()` Statements**: The simplest and most effective debugging tool is to add **print statements** in your code to track variables and the flow of the program. By printing out values of variables or messages at different stages of the program, you can quickly pinpoint where things go wrong.

Example of using **print statements**:

python

```
def player_move():
    print(f"Player             position:
{player_rect.x},  {player_rect.y}")        #
Debug the player's position
    # Move player logic here
    if
player_rect.colliderect(obstacle_rect):
        print("Collision  detected!")    #
Check for collision
```

This technique helps you track the state of variables and verify that your code is behaving as expected.

2. **Using Pygame's Built-In Debugging Tools**: Pygame provides useful tools to help with debugging:
   - **`pygame.draw.rect()`**: Draw a rectangle on the screen to visually see the player's position, boundaries, or other key elements.

215

- ○ **`pygame.time.get_ticks()`**: Track how much time has passed during the game, which is useful for debugging timers or time-dependent behaviors.

Example of **drawing the player's hitbox** for debugging:

python

```
pygame.draw.rect(screen, (255, 0, 0),
player_rect, 2)  # Draw a red border around
the player's hitbox
```

3. **Using a Debugger**: Python's built-in debugger, **pdb**, allows you to step through your code and inspect variables interactively. You can set breakpoints, step through each line, and evaluate the state of your program in real-time.

To use pdb, insert the following line where you want to start the debugger:

python

```
import pdb; pdb.set_trace()
```

This will pause the execution at that point, allowing you to enter commands to inspect the state of the program.

4. **Exception Handling**: Python provides **try-except** blocks to catch and handle errors gracefully. You can use exception handling to manage known errors and prevent crashes during gameplay.

Example of **exception handling**:

```python
try:
    result = 10 / user_input  # Division by user input
except ZeroDivisionError:
    print("Error: Cannot divide by zero!")
except ValueError:
    print("Error: Invalid input!")
```

This prevents the game from crashing if the user inputs invalid data or causes a divide-by-zero error.

Common Errors in Game Development and How to Fix Them

1. **Off-By-One Errors**: Off-by-one errors occur when you incorrectly handle indexing or looping, leading to unintended behavior. For example, accessing an array element that is outside of its range can cause the game to crash.

217

How to fix: Always ensure you are correctly indexing arrays and lists, especially when working with grids or arrays that represent game objects.

Example of fixing an off-by-one error:

python

```
# Accessing the last element in a list
correct_index = len(my_list) - 1
print(my_list[correct_index])
```

2. **Collision Detection Issues**: Collision detection is a common area for errors. If your collision detection logic is incorrect, it may result in the player passing through objects or unintended interactions.

   How to fix: Double-check the **hitboxes** of sprites, the use of **colliderect()**, and make sure that objects' **rectangles** are positioned and sized correctly.

   Example of fixing collision detection:

   python

```
if player_rect.colliderect(obstacle_rect):
    player_rect.x -= 10   # Move the player
back if they collide with an obstacle
```

3. **Performance Problems**: As the game gets more complex with multiple assets, enemies, and sprites, performance can become an issue. You may encounter **frame rate drops** or **lag** due to inefficient code.

How to fix: Use techniques like **sprite culling**, **optimizing asset sizes**, and **reducing unnecessary updates** to improve performance.

Example of **sprite culling**:

python

```
# Only update and draw objects within the
camera's view
if player_rect.colliderect(camera_rect):
    player.update()
    player.draw(screen)
```

Writing Unit Tests for Game Components

Unit tests are small tests that check individual components of your game to ensure they function as expected. While games are complex, unit tests can be written for core components such as **movement**, **collision detection**, and **game logic**.

1. **Setting Up Unit Tests**: Python's **unittest** module is a built-in tool that allows you to write tests for your game's functions.

Example of writing a unit test for **player movement**:

```python
import unittest

class
TestPlayerMovement(unittest.TestCase):
    def test_move_right(self):
        player = Player()  # Create a new
player
        player.move_right()  # Move the
player to the right
        self.assertEqual(player.rect.x,
100)  # Check if the player's position is
correct


    def test_move_left(self):
        player = Player()  # Create a new
player
        player.move_left()  # Move the
player to the left
        self.assertEqual(player.rect.x, -
100)  # Check if the player's position is
correct
```

2. **Running the Tests**: To run the tests, you can execute the test script, and it will automatically run all of the tests defined in the `TestPlayerMovement` class.

Example of running the tests:

```bash
python -m unittest test_player_movement.py
```

If any tests fail, the error messages will help you debug the issues.

Running the Game Through Different Test Scenarios

To ensure your game works under various conditions, it's essential to test it in different **scenarios** and edge cases. These scenarios might include:

1. **Testing Edge Cases**: Test the game with extreme input values, such as:
    - **Maximum score**: Does the game handle large numbers?
    - **High-speed movement**: Does the game run smoothly even with fast player or enemy speeds?
2. **Testing Different Screen Resolutions**: Test your game on various screen sizes and aspect ratios. Ensure that your

game adapts to different window sizes, and UI components scale correctly.

3. **Testing with Multiple Players**: If your game supports multiplayer, test how the game performs with multiple players, ensuring there are no conflicts, desynchronization issues, or performance drops.

Conclusion

In this chapter, we explored how to effectively **debug** and **test** your game to ensure its stability and smooth performance. We covered various debugging techniques, such as using **print statements**, **Pygame's debugging tools**, and **Python's pdb debugger**. We also discussed common game development errors and how to fix them, such as **collision detection issues, off-by-one errors**, and **performance problems**.

By writing **unit tests** for your game components and running your game through different test scenarios, you can identify and fix bugs before they impact the player's experience. Proper testing and debugging will make your game more stable, enjoyable, and free of frustrating errors. In the next chapters, we'll continue refining your game by adding advanced features, improving gameplay mechanics, and polishing the overall experience.

CHAPTER 24

DEPLOYING YOUR GAME

In this chapter, we will walk through the process of **deploying** your Python game, allowing you to **distribute** it to players across different platforms. This includes **packaging** your game for distribution, **exporting it for different platforms** (Windows, macOS, Linux), **creating an installer**, and **sharing your game** with the community. By the end of this chapter, you'll know how to make your game easily accessible and ready for players to download and enjoy.

Packaging Your Python Game for Distribution

Before distributing your game, you need to package it into a format that is easy for players to download and run. Python games often rely on external libraries (like Pygame), so it's essential to **bundle these dependencies** together with the game.

1. **Using `PyInstaller` to Package Your Game**: `PyInstaller` is a tool that allows you to bundle your Python script into an **executable** file. This is important because players won't need to install Python or external libraries to run your game.

To use `PyInstaller`, follow these steps:

1. **Install PyInstaller**: Open your terminal or command prompt and run:

bash

```
pip install pyinstaller
```

2. **Create an Executable**: Once `PyInstaller` is installed, navigate to your game's directory and run:

bash

```
pyinstaller --onefile --windowed
your_game_script.py
```

The `--onefile` option ensures that everything is bundled into a single executable file, and the `--windowed` option suppresses the terminal window from appearing when running graphical games (useful for GUI-based games).

3. **Locate the Executable**: After running the above command, `PyInstaller` will create a `dist` folder in your game's directory. Inside the `dist`

folder, you will find the **executable file** for your game.

2. **Handling Dependencies**: If your game relies on external files (like images, sounds, or configuration files), you need to ensure these files are packaged with the game. PyInstaller can include these files if you specify them in a **spec file**.

Example of adding files to the package:

bash

```
pyinstaller --add-data "assets/*;assets" -
-onefile --windowed your_game_script.py
```

This command will include all files from the assets/ directory into the executable.

Exporting the Game for Different Platforms (Windows, macOS, Linux)

Once your game is packaged into an executable, you can export it to **different platforms**. Each platform (Windows, macOS, Linux) has specific requirements for packaging and distribution.

1. **Windows**: When you run PyInstaller on Windows, the generated executable will be a .exe file. This file can

225

be run on other Windows computers without needing Python installed.

- o Ensure your game is fully tested on Windows before distribution.
- o You can use **Inno Setup** or **NSIS** to create an installer for the `.exe` file.

2. **macOS**: Packaging for macOS requires a few additional steps. You'll need to **sign your application** to avoid warnings when users run it for the first time.

To package for macOS:

- o First, ensure you are on a macOS system or use a **virtual machine** running macOS.
- o Use `PyInstaller` as described earlier to create a `.app` package.
- o After packaging, sign your application using your **Apple Developer ID** and ensure it is notarized by Apple for a smoother experience on modern macOS versions.

Example of creating a macOS package:

```bash

pyinstaller --onefile --windowed --add-data "assets/*:assets" your_game_script.py
```

You can then distribute the `.app` file or create a `.dmg` disk image for easier distribution.

3. **Linux**: Packaging for Linux is similar to Windows, but Linux doesn't use `.exe` files. Instead, you'll create a **binary** file that can be executed on Linux systems.

Example of creating a Linux executable:

```bash
```

```
pyinstaller --onefile --windowed --add-data "assets/*:assets" your_game_script.py
```

- o The output will be a **binary** file that can be run directly on Linux.
- o To make the game easier to install, you can create a **.deb** package (for Debian-based distributions) or a **.rpm** package (for Red Hat-based distributions).

Creating an Installer for Your Game

An **installer** allows users to easily set up your game on their system. It typically installs the game files, adds shortcuts, and ensures all dependencies are included.

1. **Creating an Installer for Windows**: To create a Windows installer, you can use tools like **Inno Setup** or **NSIS (Nullsoft Scriptable Install System)**.

   Example using **Inno Setup**:

   o Download and install **Inno Setup** from here.
   o Create a script for your installer, specifying the files to be included (such as the executable and assets).
   o Compile the script to create an installer .exe file.

2. **Creating an Installer for macOS**: For macOS, you can create a .dmg **disk image** or .pkg **installer**.

   o Use **create-dmg** (a command-line tool) to create .dmg files that package your app.
   o Alternatively, you can use **Packages** (a graphical tool) to create .pkg files for easy installation.

3. **Creating an Installer for Linux**: For Linux, you can create .deb or .rpm packages using tools like **dpkg** or **rpm**.

   o For Debian-based systems, create a .deb package that users can install using the package manager (dpkg or apt).
   o For Red Hat-based systems, create a .rpm package.

You can also use **AppImage** for distributing a single executable file that works across many Linux distributions.

Sharing Your Game with the Community

Once your game is packaged and ready for distribution, you can share it with the community through various platforms.

1. **Uploading to Game Distribution Platforms**:

    o **itch.io**: A popular platform for indie games where you can upload your game and set a price or offer it for free.

    o **Steam**: The biggest game distribution platform. Steam offers tools for indie developers to publish their games, though the process requires a **developer account** and **approval**.

    o **GOG (Good Old Games)**: Another platform for distributing DRM-free games.

    o **Game Jolt**: A platform that allows you to share your games with the community and receive feedback.

2. **Using GitHub for Open-Source Games**: If your game is open-source or you want to make the source code publicly available, **GitHub** is a great place to host it. You can use

GitHub Releases to distribute the compiled executable files alongside the source code.

3. **Sharing Through Social Media**: Share updates, trailers, and links to your game on social media platforms such as Twitter, Facebook, and Reddit. Engaging with the community through regular updates can help attract attention to your game.

Conclusion

In this chapter, we covered the process of **deploying** your Python game, focusing on:

- **Packaging** your game for distribution using **PyInstaller**.
- **Exporting** the game for different platforms such as **Windows**, **macOS**, and **Linux**.
- **Creating an installer** for your game, making it easy for players to install.
- **Sharing your game** with the community through platforms like **itch.io**, **Steam**, and **GitHub**.

By following these steps, your game will be ready to reach a wider audience. Whether you're targeting PC, macOS, or Linux, deploying your game is an essential step in making it accessible and enjoyable for players everywhere.

CHAPTER 25

INTRODUCTION TO GAME DEVELOPMENT WITH PYGAME ZERO

In this chapter, we will explore **Pygame Zero**, a simplified framework built on top of **Pygame** that is designed to make game development easier for beginners. Pygame Zero reduces the complexity of writing games by abstracting away much of the boilerplate code required in Pygame, allowing you to focus on the game logic. Whether you are new to game development or want to make a small project quickly, Pygame Zero is an excellent tool to get started with making games.

What is Pygame Zero and How It Differs from Pygame

Pygame Zero is a game development library for beginners, designed to allow quick and easy creation of 2D games. It is built on top of **Pygame**, which is a popular library for creating 2D games in Python. The key difference between Pygame and Pygame Zero is that Pygame Zero simplifies the process of setting up a game by providing a set of pre-defined functions and a simplified structure.

231

Here's how **Pygame Zero** differs from **Pygame**:

1. **No Need for `pygame.init()` or a Game Loop**: Pygame Zero eliminates the need to manually initialize Pygame with `pygame.init()` and creates a default game loop for you. This makes it easier for beginners to start coding without worrying about complex setup.

2. **Simple   Structure**: Instead of requiring complex classes, event handling, and manual updates of screen displays, Pygame Zero allows you to focus on defining actions and behavior in a few simple functions like `draw()` and `update()`. These are automatically called by Pygame Zero during the game loop.

3. **Automatic   Screen   Setup**: Pygame Zero automatically sets up a window for your game, so you don't need to manually create a display or set up screen dimensions.

4. **Built-In   Game   Elements**: It provides built-in support for common game elements like **images**, **sounds**, and **sprite movement**, allowing you to get started more quickly.

Setting Up a Simple Game with Pygame Zero

Getting started with Pygame Zero is very simple. You can set up a basic game with just a few lines of code. Here's how to create a simple **moving sprite** game where the player controls a character.

1. **Installation**: Before we begin, make sure that **Pygame Zero** is installed on your system. You can install it using pip:

   bash

   ```
   pip install pgzero
   ```

2. **Setting Up a Simple Game**: To start, create a new Python file (e.g., my_game.py). This is where you'll write your game code. Here's a basic example:

   python

   ```
   # Import Pygame Zero library
   import pgzrun

   # Define a global variable for the player's
   position
   player  =  Actor("character_image")    #
   Replace  "character_image"  with  an  image
   file (PNG/JPG)
   ```

```
# Initial position of the player
player.x = 100
player.y = 100

# Update function (called every frame)
def update():
    if keyboard.left:
        player.x -= 5  # Move left
    if keyboard.right:
        player.x += 5  # Move right
    if keyboard.up:
        player.y -= 5  # Move up
    if keyboard.down:
        player.y += 5  # Move down

# Draw function (called every frame)
def draw():
    screen.fill((255, 255, 255))  # Fill
the screen with a white background
    player.draw()  # Draw the player
character on the screen

# Run the game
```

pgzrun.go()

vbnet

3. **Explanation**:

234

- The `Actor()` function loads an image for the player character. You can use any `.png` or `.jpg` image that is in the same directory as your Python script.
- The `update()` function moves the player using the arrow keys (left, right, up, down).
- The `draw()` function draws the player on the screen, refreshing every frame.
- Finally, the `pgzrun.go()` function runs the game, and the game loop is automatically set up by Pygame Zero.

4. **Running the Game**:
- Save your game file and run it using `pgzrun` from the terminal:
   ```bash
   pgzrun my_game.py
   ```
- Your game will open in a window, and you can move the character using the arrow keys.

Benefits of Using Pygame Zero for Beginners

Pygame Zero is an excellent tool for beginners for several reasons:

235

1. **No Boilerplate Code**:
Pygame Zero simplifies the setup process, removing the need to deal with initialization, screen setup, and complex event handling. This allows you to focus more on the creative aspects of game development without getting bogged down in technical details.

2. **Simplified Syntax**:
Pygame Zero uses a simple, intuitive syntax that is easier for beginners to learn. For example, handling **keyboard input** is as simple as checking for `keyboard.left`, `keyboard.right`, etc. You don't need to manually handle events like in Pygame.

3. **Fast Prototyping**:
Since it reduces the complexity of creating games, you can quickly prototype your ideas and experiment with gameplay mechanics. You can also easily replace or modify assets like images and sounds.

4. **Clear Game Loop**:
Pygame Zero takes care of the **game loop** (where `update()` and `draw()` are called automatically), which can be confusing for beginners working with Pygame. This abstraction makes it easier to focus on gameplay design.

5. **Great for Learning**:
Because of its simplicity, Pygame Zero is ideal for beginners who want to learn basic game development concepts, like movement, collision detection, and game loops, without being overwhelmed by the complexities of traditional game engines.

Creating Your First Game Without Complex Code

Pygame Zero allows you to create simple yet functional games with minimal code. Here's an example of how you can create a **simple click-to-destroy game** where the player clicks on an enemy to destroy it:

```python
# Import the Pygame Zero library
import pgzrun

# Create the player character (a simple circle
for this example)
player = Actor("player_image")
player.x = 100
player.y = 100
```

```python
# Create an enemy character
enemy = Actor("enemy_image")
enemy.x = 300
enemy.y = 100


# Update function to move the player
def update():
 if keyboard.left:
    player.x -= 5
 if keyboard.right:
    player.x += 5
 if keyboard.up:
    player.y -= 5
 if keyboard.down:
    player.y += 5


 # Check if the player clicks on the enemy
 if player.collidepoint(mouse.x, mouse.y) and
mouse.is_pressed():
    enemy.x = 600  # Move the enemy off-screen
when destroyed

# Draw function to display the game
def draw():
 screen.fill((255, 255, 255))  # White background
 player.draw()
 enemy.draw()
```

```
# Start the game loop
pgzrun.go()
```

In this game:

- The player can move the character with the arrow keys.
- When the player clicks on the enemy (if the mouse is over the enemy sprite), the enemy is "destroyed" by moving it off-screen.

This example demonstrates how easy it is to create interactive games in Pygame Zero with minimal code, making it perfect for learning game development concepts without getting bogged down in complexity.

Conclusion

In this chapter, we introduced **Pygame Zero**, a simplified framework that is built on top of **Pygame** and designed for beginners. We explored the advantages of using Pygame Zero, such as its **simplicity**, **easy setup**, and **reduced boilerplate code**, which allows you to quickly create 2D games. We also covered how to set up a basic game with Pygame Zero, move a character, and create interactive gameplay with minimal coding.

Pygame Zero is an excellent starting point for newcomers to game development, providing a simple and intuitive environment to learn key concepts like sprite movement, collision detection, and game loops. Once you're comfortable with Pygame Zero, you can gradually move on to more advanced game engines and frameworks, but it will always be a great tool for rapid prototyping and creating simple games.

In the next chapters, you can expand your knowledge by adding more complex mechanics, such as **power-ups**, **enemies**, and **game levels**, while continuing to enjoy the simplicity of Pygame Zero. Happy game developing!

www.ingramcontent.com/pod-product-compliance
Lightning Source LLC
La Vergne TN
LVHW022340060326
832902LV00022B/4145